Popular Teaching Resources

Art Lessons

Grades 1-2

Anita Law • Monica Whatley

Contents

Drama and Dance

Checklists

Project Ideas

Guidelines for Use

This resource book contains three sections:

- Core Units
- Checklists
- Project Ideas

Each **Core Unit** is made up of an information sheet, two follow-up worksheets, and an activity for the entire class to do together. You will see that in all of the units, "Name", "Date", and the unit topic appear in each follow-up worksheet so that each one can stand on its own. There is more than one way to present each unit in the book. Here are two that may work for you: (1) give your students the lesson and the worksheets at the same time and let them work on both simultaneously, followed by the class activity; (2) give just the lesson and class activity one day and ask your students to underline key words and ideas or take notes as you talk about the subject, and then give them a worksheet the next day as a quiz.

The **Checklists** allow both you and your students to mark the students' progress and recognize which areas may need more study or attention.

The **Project Ideas** give students the opportunity to work creatively on projects that will help them develop their understanding of the material in many of the Core Units.

Happy teaching!

Art Lessons
Grades 1-2

Music

Beat...Beat...Beat

Objective: *To identify examples of beat in daily life and in music*

What sound does a clock make? *Tick, tock, tick, tock...* **How does your heart sound?** *Thump, thump, thump, thump...* **We call it a heartbeat because its thumping is steady and even.**

In music, this steady pulse is the **beat** of a song. In a big marching band, there is always someone with a drum carrying the beat, hitting it with a "bam, bam, bam".

When you clap your hands along to a song, you clap the beat. Can you hear the beat in this song?

We clap on the words in bold. This is the beat of the song.

Yankee **Doo**dle **went** to **town**
Riding **on** a **po-ny**
Stuck a **fea**ther **in** his **cap**
And **called** it **ma**ca**ro-ni!**

Poems and rhymes we read sound like they have a beat, too. Try clapping along to this one:

Rain on the **green grass** and **rain on** the **tree**
And **rain on** the **housetops** but **not on me**.

Where else can you hear a steady beat around you?

                          Art Lessons | G.1 & 2

Beat...Beat...Beat

Recite the song and clap the
beats. Then circle the words
you clapped.

*The first two lines are done for you.
Trace the circles and complete the
rest of the song.*

(Mary) (had) a (little) (lamb),

(Little) (lamb), (little) (lamb),

Mary had a little lamb,

Whose fleece was white as snow.

And everywhere that Mary went,

Mary went, Mary went,

And everywhere that Mary went,

The lamb was sure to go.

Beat...Beat...Beat

Choose a movement that you want to accompany each rhyme. Then cut it out and glue it in the space next to the rhyme. Perform the movements to the beat of each rhyme with your class.

Star Light, Star Bright

Star light, star bright,

The first star I see tonight,

I wish I may, I wish I might,

Have the wish I wish tonight.

Deedle Deedle Dumpling

Deedle, deedle, dumpling, my son John

Went to bed with his stockings on,

One shoe off, one shoe on.

Deedle, deedle, dumpling, my son John.

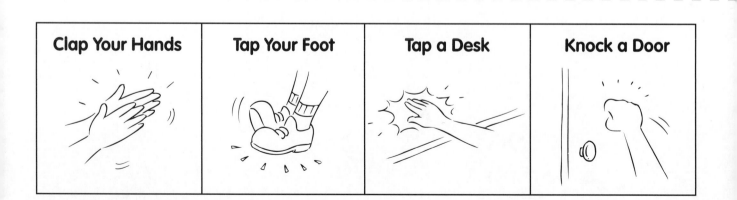

| Clap Your Hands | Tap Your Foot | Tap a Desk | Knock a Door |

Beat...Beat...Beat

Beating to Our Own Drum

Materials:

- large empty coffee can or margarine container with lid
- thin fabric with interesting print
- rubber band
- construction paper
- metal spoons

Motivation:

To *make individual drums and practise identifying the beat in rhymes and songs*

What to Do:

Part 1: Make the Drum

1. Place the can face down onto a piece of fabric. Draw a circle 3 cm larger than the rim. Cut this out.

2. Place the can on its side on the construction paper. Mark the paper along the edges of the drum. Crease along these lines and cut.

3. Decorate the paper using stickers, markers, cut outs, etc.

4. Glue the construction paper around the can.

5. Place the fabric over the lid of the drum, securing it with a rubber band.

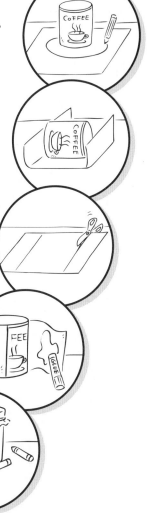

Part 2: Beat the Drum

1. Practise beating the drum with the metal spoons. See if everyone can join in on the beat, "Bam, bam, bam, bam...".

2. Sing and play the beat of *Apples and Bananas* or any other song or rhyme you use in class.

I Got Rhythm

Objective: *To identify rhythmic patterns and distinguish between beat and rhythm in a simple song*

Tah dum, tah dum, tah dum...

Tah deedle de dum, tah dum!

The first line sounds like the steady beat you might hear from a drum. The second is a little different: it moves ahead a little faster and makes a rhythm.

Rhythm is not a steady beat; it is a pattern of long and short sounds that drives the music forward. If you listen carefully, you might be able to hear the different rhythms all around you. Listen to your grandmother's knitting needles go *click, click, swirl*. Maybe there's a rhythm to your mom's vegetable chopping as well.

Both poems and songs have rhythm. Slowly clap the syllables of this nursery rhyme.

Hick-or-y dick-or-y dock

The mouse ran up the clock

The clock struck one

The mouse ran down

Hick-or-y dick-or-y dock.

10   Art Lessons | G.1 & 2

I Got Rhythm

Make the rhythm with each musical instrument by following the given description. Then create a rhythm of your own.

1.

They make a "sha" sound.

Maracas

A Rhythm: sha... sha... sha sha...

sha... sha... sha sha...

My Own Rhythm: _____

_____

2.

They make a "tak" sound.

Castanets

A Rhythm: tak tak tak... tak... tak

tak tak tak... tak... tak

My Own Rhythm: _____

_____

I Got Rhythm

Do this activity with a partner. Clap out the rhythm of one of the songs below and have your partner guess which song you are clapping. Colour a box each time your partner gets the answer correct. Play ten times and see who knows the rhythm of the songs best.

Happy Birthday to You

Happy birthday to you,

Happy birthday to you,

Happy birthday to you,

Happy birthday to you.

London Bridge Is Falling Down

London Bridge is falling down,

Falling down, falling down.

London Bridge is falling down,

My fair lady.

Your Partner's Record*

Number of Times Correct

*After playing, cut out this portion and give it to your partner.

I Got Rhythm

Maracas

Motivation:

To accompany songs, using appropriate rhythm instruments, body percussion, or "found" instruments

Materials:

- empty water bottles with lids
- popcorn kernels or rice
- tissue paper (various colours)
- white glue (and water)
- paintbrushes – thick
- paper plate or tray
- scissors

What to Do:

1 Cut the tissue paper into 3-cm squares.

2 Add a little water to a plate of white glue to make a glue wash.

3 Paint a portion of the water bottle with the glue wash and cover it with the tissue paper squares. Overlap the squares in different colours.

4 Paint the decorated bottle with the glue wash as a varnish and allow to dry.

5 Add kernels or rice to the bottle, until it is about 1/3 full and seal the opening.

6 Pair up the students. Have each student shake out a simple rhythm and see if his or her partner can repeat it.

7 Shake the maracas to the rhythm of *Skinnamarink* or *Hokey Pokey* and point out that even their names have a rhythm!

Let's Pitch in!

Objective: To identify higher and lower pitched sounds in their environment and in music

What does a bird's chirp sound like?

How about the rumbling of the thunder?

Music is made up of all sorts of sounds. Some are very high, like a bird's song, and others are low, like the deep rumble of thunder. The highness or lowness of a tone is called its **pitch**.

What different pitches can you hear outside, at home, or at the grocery store?

Pitch can slide up or down, slowly or quickly. Your voice changes pitch just like a cart on a roller coaster. How would your voice sound if it started low and slowly got higher and then quickly dropped down again?

Composers, or music writers, use symbols or notes to show a change in pitch. This allows *anybody* to play the songs that they have written.

Your voice can rise and fall, just like a roller coaster!

Let's Pitch in!

Imitate the sound of each animal. Then write whether it is "high pitched" or "low pitched" on the line.

1.

Oink, oink!

_____

2.

Woof, woof!

_____

3.

Chirp, chirp!

_____

4.

Moo, moo!

_____

5.

...hiss...

6.

Quack, quack!

_____

7.

...meow, meow...

_____

_____

Name: _____   Date: _____

Let's Pitch in!

Draw a picture of yourself in the circle. Colour the boxes to show the pitch of your voice, and those of your family members and friends.

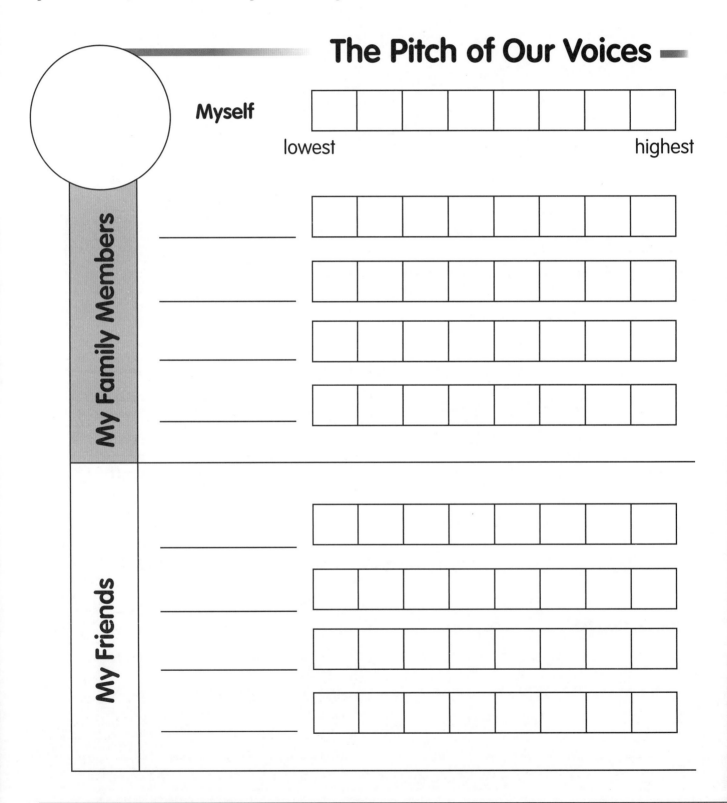

The Pitch of Our Voices

Myself

lowest   highest

My Family Members

My Friends

Let's Pitch in!

Singing out

Materials:

- three glass cups
- water
- metal spoons

Motivation:

To demonstrate an understanding of high and low pitches

What to Do:

Hit the glass gently, please.

Activity 1: Tapping Glasses

1 Fill one glass with water, another half full, and leave the last glass empty.

2 Allow the students to tap the glasses lightly with a metal spoon.

3 Discuss the pitch that each glass has when it is tapped.

Which glass has the highest pitch?

Which glass has the lowest pitch?

4 Add water to or remove water from each to see how the pitch changes.

Activity 2: Giraffes and Ants

1 Have a student play or sing a pitch.

2 Depending on the pitch, the other students should move around like a "giraffe" stretching as high as they can, or like an ant, as low as possible.

Now That's Dynamic!

Objective: To identify examples of dynamics in the environment and in music

zzz-ZZZ-zzz-ZZZ-zzz-ZZZ-zzz-ZZZ-zzz-ZZZ

When you hear someone snoring, is it always loud? Or does it start off quietly and grow louder, and then quiet down again?

The loudness and softness of music are its **dynamics**. By making music softer or louder in different parts, you can make it more interesting and give it different feelings. Sing *I'm a Little Teapot* with different dynamics:

I'm a Little Teapot

I'm a little tea pot
Short and stout
Here is my handle
Here is my spout
When I get all steamed up
Hear me shout:
Tip me over
And pour me out!
I'm a very special pot
It's true
Here's an example
Of what I can do
I can change my
handle and my spout
Then tip me over and
Pour me out.

Tip Me Over and Pour Me Out!

You can show the dynamics of a song using your arms. Make big movements, like a conductor of a symphony, when the music gets loud. As the music quiets, make your arm movements smaller and smaller!

Now That's Dynamic!

Do this activity with a partner. Make sound with the indicated instruments and write the sound in words. Write the words in sizes that match the given dynamics.

Dynamics: soft, soft, loud, loud

boom, boom, **boom, boom**

1. **Boom Boom!** Dynamics: loud, soft, soft, soft

Sound:

2. **Ding Ding!** Dynamics: soft, loud, loud, soft, soft

Sound:

3. **Sha Sha!** Dynamics: loud, soft, soft, loud, soft, loud

Sound:

Now That's Dynamic!

Check the noises that have different sound dynamics.

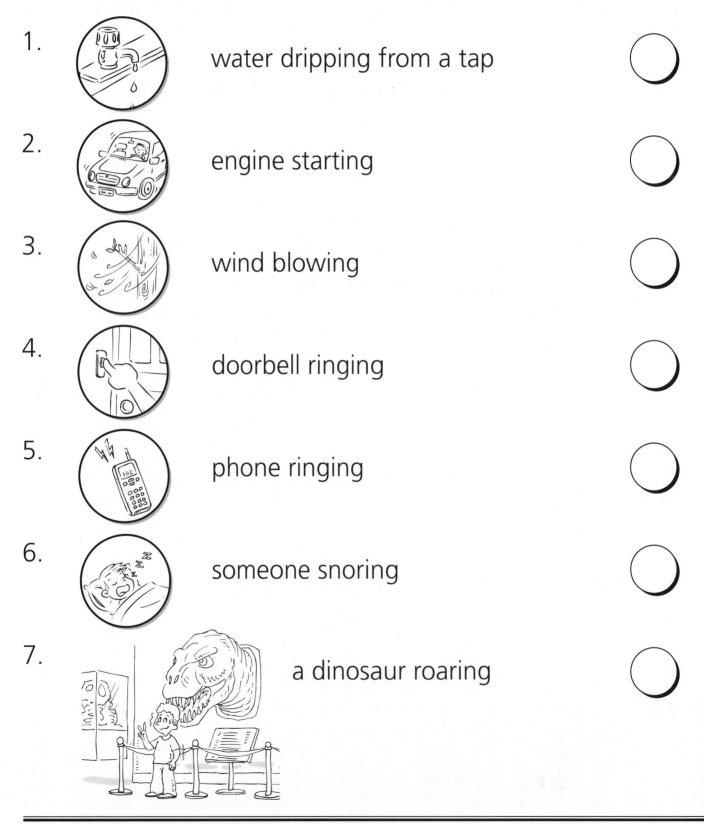

1. water dripping from a tap ◯

2. engine starting ◯

3. wind blowing ◯

4. doorbell ringing ◯

5. phone ringing ◯

6. someone snoring ◯

7. a dinosaur roaring ◯

Now That's Dynamic!

Loud and Soft

Motivation:

To *identify examples of dynamics in pieces of music and show how loudness and softness are achieved*

What to Do:

1 Experiment with the instruments.

- How can you make a quiet, calm sound?
- Which instrument could you use to wake someone up?

2 Listen to Debussy's *Golliwog's Cakewalk* and Sergei Prokofiev's *Peter and the Wolf*. Pay attention to their dynamics.

- How does loudness and softness change the feeling of the music?
- What kind of sounds are heard? (bang, crash, ding, etc.)

3 Let the students know that they can add their own dynamics to music. Use the instruments to recite *Go Bananas* together and increase and decrease the volume.

4 Have everyone sing various songs and experiment with the volume to change the feeling (e.g. *Good Night, Ladies*, *Jingle Bells*, *Down By The Bay*, etc.)

Go bananas!
Go go bananas!
Go bananas!
Go go bananas!

Tempo Time

Objective: To identify the tempo in the environment and in music

When your heart is beating normally, it is a slow, steady, even beat: *Thump...* *Thump...* *Thump...* **When you start jumping or running, the beat speeds up:** *Thump. Thump. Thump.*

In music, we call a change in the speed of a tune a change in **tempo**. Music can be fast or slow, or change back and forth throughout. A fast tempo might make you feel happy or lively. A slow tempo might make you feel tired or sad.

You can show the tempo of a musical piece using your arms. Listen to Khachaturian's *Sabre Dance*. Move your arms slowly or quickly according to the tempo of the music!

Let's sing *Head and Shoulders* faster and faster while doing the actions.

Head and Shoulders

Head and shoulders, knees and toes, knees and toes, knees and toes,

Head and shoulders, knees and toes,

Eyes, ears, mouth, and nose.

Ankles, elbows, feet, and seat, feet and seat, feet and seat,

Ankles, elbows, feet, and seat,

Hair, hips, chin, and cheeks.

Head and shoulders, knees...

Now let's slow it down. Are the actions easier to do now? Try this with *A Ram Sam Sam* or *My Aunt Came Back*.

Tempo Time

Sing each song with a different tempo. Circle the tempo that you think is most appropriate. Then write how you feel when you sing the song with that tempo.

B-I-N-G-O

There was a farmer had a dog,

And Bingo was his name O.

B-I-N-G-O

B-I-N-G-O

B-I-N-G-O

And Bingo was his name O.

- Tempo: slow / medium / fast

- How I feel: _____

Rock-A-Bye Baby

Rock-A-Bye baby

In the treetop

When the wind blows

The cradle will rock

When the bough breaks

The cradle will fall

And down will come baby

Cradle and all

- Tempo: slow / medium / fast

- How I feel: _____

Tempo Time

Write the name and the lyrics of your favourite song below. Then circle the tempo you think is best for that song.

Name of the Song:

Tempo: slow / medium / fast

Tempo Time

The Bumblebee

Motivation:

To demonstrate that music can be played fast or slow and that changes in tempo give the listener different feelings

<table>
<tr><td>Materials:

• Flight of the Bumblebee by Rimsky-Korsakov
• crayons of various colours
• 8 x 10" white Bristol board</td></tr>
</table>

What to Do:

1 Have the students colour the bee with crayons and cut it out.

2 Discuss how music can create a picture in the listener's mind.

3 With everyone's eyes closed, play *Flight of the Bumblebee*. Have the students pretend that they are the bee and imagine the bee's flight.

- What does the bee see along the way?

- Where does it stop?

4 Have the students start tracing the flight of the bee at one end of the Bristol board and draw its path in crayon. Encourage them to make the path flip and turn, until it reaches the other end of the Bristol board.

5 Paste the bee at the end of its path.

In the Family (I)

Objective: *To identify the four families of orchestral instruments*

Think of your family. Do you have any brothers or sisters? How about an aunt or a grandpa living with you?

The instruments have families, too. You can see that certain instruments are related to one another, as they are often alike. They are made of the same materials, and make sound in the same way.

These are the four instrument families:

Brass

• They have a pipe at one end and a bell at the other.

• You make a buzzing sound into the mouthpiece and press the buttons to change the pitch.

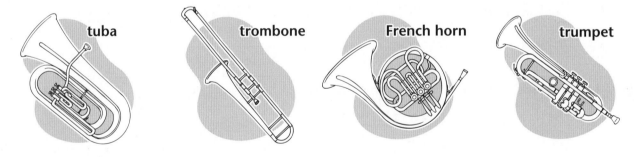

tuba   trombone   French horn   trumpet

Percussion

• You hit, scrape, or shake these instruments to change the pitch or play the beat or the rhythm.

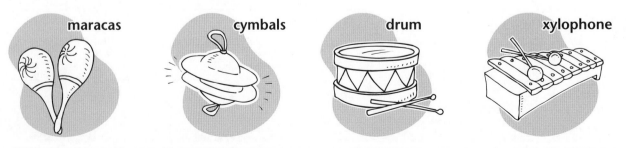

maracas   cymbals   drum   xylophone

       Art Lessons | G.1 & 2

In the Family (II)

String

- They are often made of wood and are hollow to let the sound of the vibrating strings get louder.

- You move a bow made of real horse tail hair across the strings to make sound or pluck the strings with your fingers.

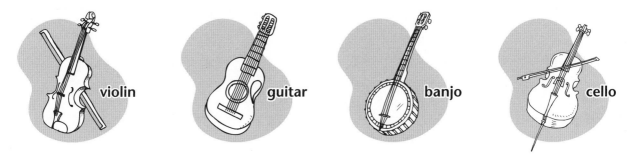

violin   guitar   banjo   cello

Woodwind

- They used to be made mostly out of wood, but can now be made of silver, nickel, or other metals.

- They are thin pipes with holes along them.

- You blow air through the mouthpiece and use your fingers to cover the holes to make sound and to change the pitch.

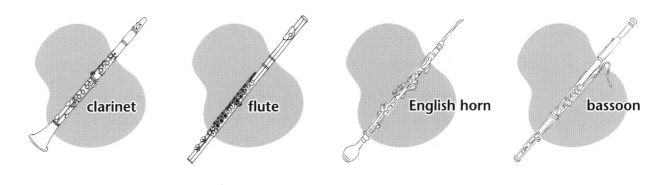

clarinet   flute   English horn   bassoon

In the Family

Draw lines to match the instrument families with the way they make sound. Then identify the musical instruments. Write the families they belong to and their names.

Instrument Family

percussion   •

string   •

brass   •

woodwind   •

• Blow into it.

• Buzz in it.

• Hit it.

• Pluck it.

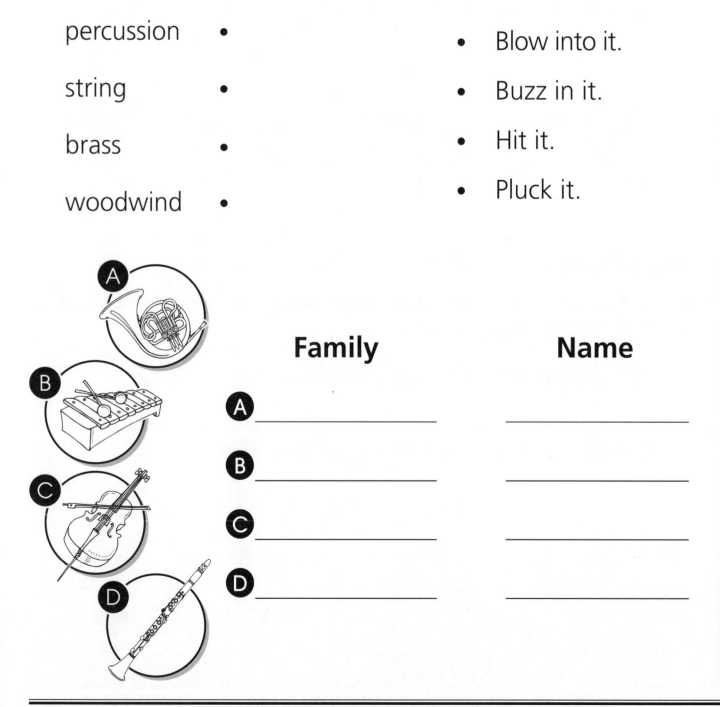

Family   **Name**

A _____   _____

B _____   _____

C _____   _____

D _____   _____

28   Art Lessons | G.1 & 2

In the Family

Making Instruments

Motivation:

To create instruments using a variety of sound sources

Materials:

- ruler
- shoebox
- glass bottle
- rubber bands
  (various widths)

What to Do:

Instrument 1

Fill a water bottle half full with water, insert a straw, and blow air into it.

Instrument 2

Hold a ruler on the edge of a desk. Push down on the other end and release.

Instrument 3

Stretch rubber bands (from thinnest to thickest) around the length of the shoebox. Space them evenly to make "strings". Pluck them with their fingers and listen to the different sounds they can make.

Follow-Up:

Have the students use these and other instruments to make their own music. Encourage them to change the tempo, dynamics, or rhythm to add excitement!

Visual Arts

Primary Colours

Objective: To identify the primary colours

Look around you. Can you name some colours you know?

Some of the colours we see around us are called primary colours. Primary means first or the most important. Primary colours are the most important colours. They can be mixed to produce all the colours of the rainbow, but they cannot be made by mixing other colours.

The **primary colours** are:

- **red**

- **yellow**

- **blue**

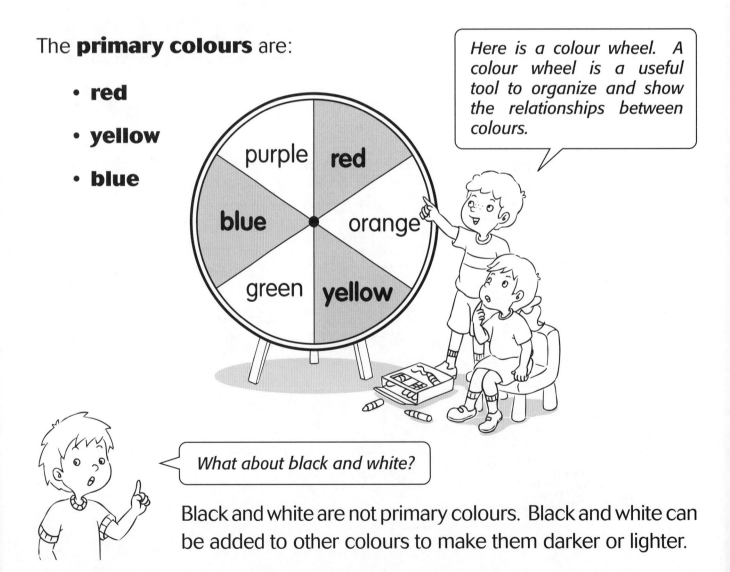

> *Here is a colour wheel. A colour wheel is a useful tool to organize and show the relationships between colours.*

> *What about black and white?*

Black and white are not primary colours. Black and white can be added to other colours to make them darker or lighter.

Primary Colours

Write the names of the primary colours on the lines. Then write your name on the T-shirt and colour it with the primary colours.

Primary Colours:

_____ , _____ , and _____

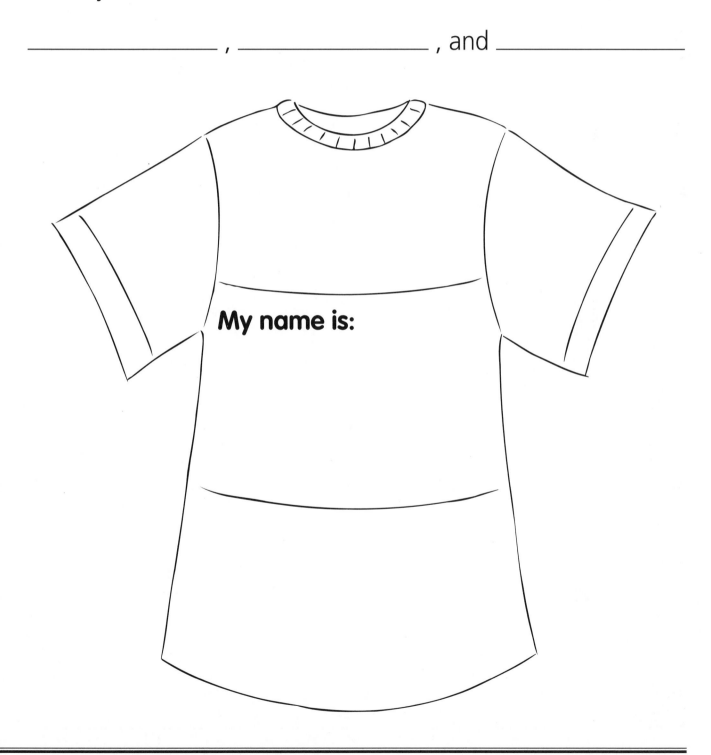

My name is:

Primary Colours

Colour the cat with colours that are not primary colours. Then colour each section of the background with the specified primary colours.

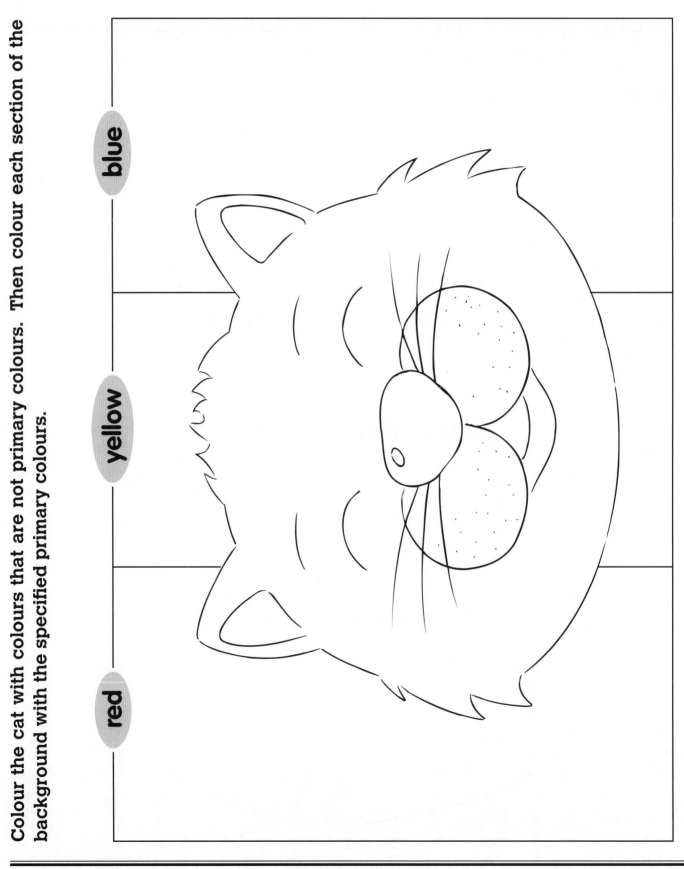

Primary Colours

Stamp It Out!

Materials:

- white construction paper
- assorted sponge shapes
- red, yellow, and blue tempera paint
- paper plates – one for each colour
- newspapers

Motivation:

To *create and expand pattern sequences* with *primary colours*

What to Do:

 Line desks with newspapers.

2 Put some paint on the paper plates.

3 Each student needs three sponge shapes and three colours.

4 Have students create their own shape-and-colour pattern sequences on the white construction paper.

Example:

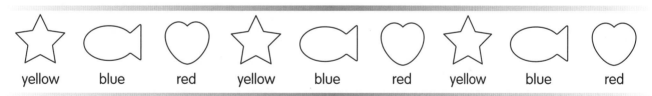

| yellow | blue | red | yellow | blue | red | yellow | blue | red |

Discussion:

Have students share their pattern sequences with the class.

Teacher Tip:

Children tend to overload the sponge with a lot of paint. Demonstrate to students how to dip the sponge lightly into the paint and then lightly press it onto the paper.

Secondary Colours

Objective: *To name the secondary colours and identify how they are created by the primary colours*

Can you tell me the names of the primary colours?

If we mix some of the primary colours, do you think they will change and make other colours?

Secondary colours are created by mixing two primary colours.

The secondary colours are:

- **purple**
- **orange**
- **green**

Can you see the secondary colours on the colour wheel?

Secondary colours are made by mixing the primary colours on either side of them. Take a look at the colour wheel again.

Can you see the primary colours on the colour wheel?

See how we use primary colours to make the secondary colours.

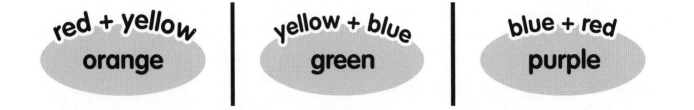

red + yellow	yellow + blue	blue + red
orange	**green**	**purple**

                    Art Lessons | G.1 & 2

Secondary Colours

Paint each circle as specified to see how to make secondary colours by mixing the primary colours on a tray. Then fill in the blanks with colour names.

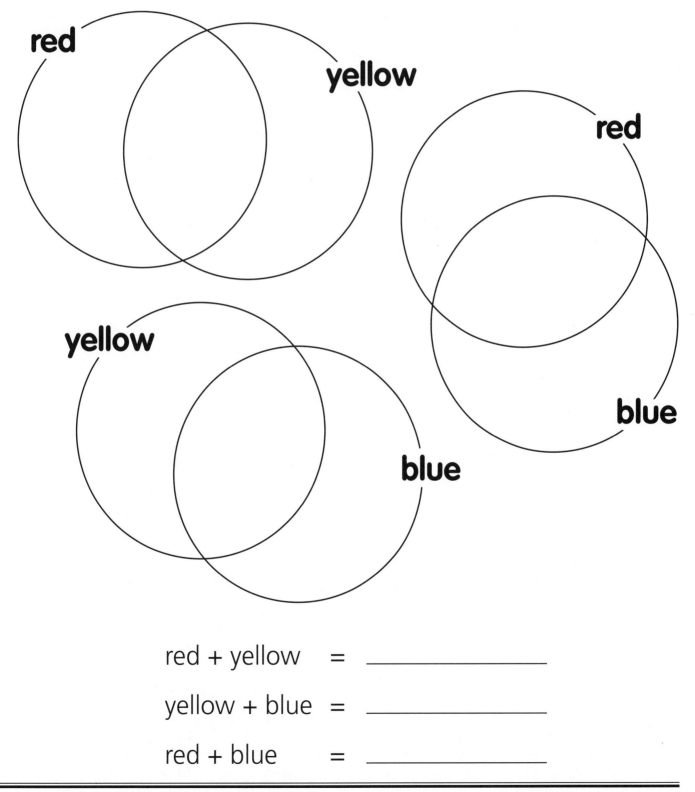

red + yellow   = _____

yellow + blue   = _____

red + blue   = _____

Secondary Colours

Answer the questions. Then colour the picture with the secondary colours.

1. Which two primary colours make purple?

   _____

2. Which two primary colours make green?

   _____

3. Which two primary colours make orange?

   _____

Secondary Colours

My Bubbly Name

Motivation:

To experiment with how secondary colours are created

Materials:

- white construction paper
- cut-out bubble letters
- red, yellow, and blue tempera paint
- paper plates – one for each colour
- paintbrushes
- water cans
- newspapers

What to Do:

1 Line desks with newspapers.

2 Each student needs one paintbrush and one water can.

3 Put some paint on the paper plates.

4 Have students trace their names on the white construction paper using the cut-out bubble letters.

5 Ask students to colour their names by using two primary colours on each letter.

Discussion:

What happens when two primary colours are mixed?

Teacher Tip:

Teach students to rinse their paintbrushes in the water can before proceeding to another colour. Demonstrate to students how a paintbrush with many colours will lead to a shade of brown.

Primary and Secondary Colours

Objective: To identify primary and secondary colours and to recall the term "rainbow"

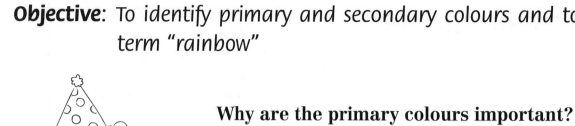

Why are the primary colours important?

Which colours are secondary colours?

Can you tell me which two primary colours are mixed to create which secondary colour?

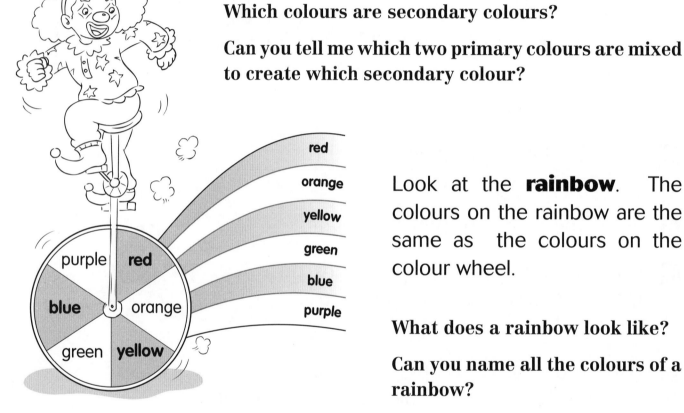

Look at the **rainbow**. The colours on the rainbow are the same as the colours on the colour wheel.

What does a rainbow look like?

Can you name all the colours of a rainbow?

A long time ago, some people believed that rainbows were magic. They believed that you could find a pot of gold at the end of a rainbow where it touched the Earth.

A rainbow is caused by sunlight shining on raindrops. This is why we often see a rainbow as the rain is tapering off and the sun is coming out again. Rainbow colours always appear in the same order: **red**, **orange**, **yellow**, **green**, **blue**, **and purple**. Rainbows are in the shape of an arch with red at the top arch and purple at the bottom arch.

Primary and Secondary Colours

Colour the rainbow.

red
orange
yellow
green
blue
purple

Primary and Secondary Colours

Colour each fruit in a rainbow of colours.

Primary and Secondary Colours

After the Rain

Materials:

- drawing paper
- crayons in the colours of the rainbow
- watered-down tempera paint
- paintbrushes
- water cans
- newspapers

Motivation:

To study and paint a rainbow using the crayon-resist technique

Crayon-resist Technique:

Colour very heavily using crayons, and then paint over the drawing with watered-down tempera paint. The crayon will resist the paint and create an interesting effect.

What to Do:

1 Line desks with newspapers.

2 Explain the crayon-resist technique to students.

3 Have students use crayons to draw and colour a rainbow. They can add their choice of other details, such as the sun, raindrops, and maybe a pot of gold!

4 Emphasize to students that for the crayon-resist process to work, they need to press down firmly when colouring.

5 Once the colouring is completed, students can paint across their paper with watered-down tempera paint.

Tints

Objective: To *describe the changes that occur when white is added to a colour*

What do you think happens when white is added to red?

When a colour is mixed with white, a lighter version of that colour is created. The lighter tone of a colour is known as a **tint**.

Look at a box of pastels. Baby blue, mellow yellow, and rose pink are examples of tints of blue, yellow, and red. They give a softer, lighter, and fresher impression than their original colours.

Let's use a flashlight and look at a piece of artwork.

How does the light affect the look of the artwork?

How does the light change the colours of the artwork?

Adding white to a colour has the same effect as shining light on a colour. The original colour becomes lighter and a tint of that colour is created.

Let me show you how to make "pink"!

Red   White

PINK
(A Tint of Red)

44   Art Lessons | G.1 & 2

Tints

Paint the whole object with the specified colour. Then paint over the part on the right with white before it dries to show a tint of that colour.

Tints

Jack is shining the flashlight onto the picture. Colour the picture. Remember to colour over the illuminated part with white to show the tints of the colours.

You can colour the entire picture first. Then colour the illuminated part again with a white pencil crayon.

Tints

Colour Creations

Motivation:

To experiment with mixing different colours with white

What to Do:

1 Pick any one of the primary colours.

2 Colour the fish with the primary colour and its tints.

3 Then add some body parts to the fish (e.g. eyes, mouth, fins, etc.) with a marker.

Materials:

- red, yellow, blue, and white pastel
- marker

My Design

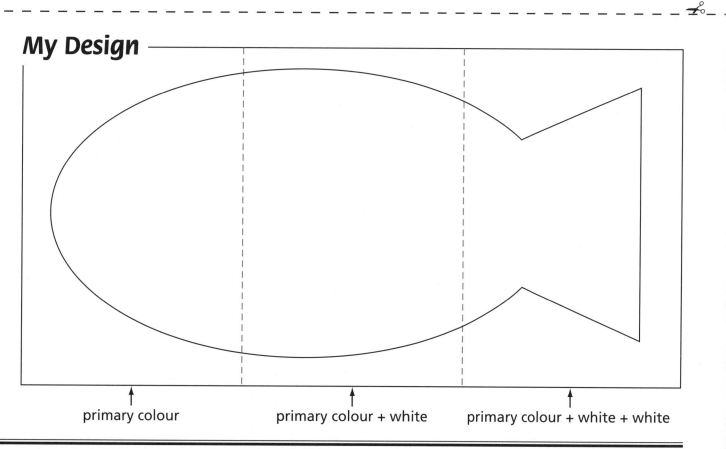

primary colour   primary colour + white   primary colour + white + white

Shades

Objective: To *describe the changes that occur when black is added to a colour*

What do you think happens when a little black is added to yellow?

When a colour is mixed with black, a darker version of that colour is produced. The darker tone of a colour is known as a **shade**.

Imagine it is summertime and you are standing outside under the scorching hot sun. Naturally, you would find a shaded area to hide from the sun and prevent yourself from getting sunburned. When you stand under the shade, everything appears less bright and less intense. Adding black to a colour has the same effect; the resulting colour is duller than the original colour.

Put on a pair of sunglasses and look at your surroundings. How do the sunglasses affect the look of the objects around you?

The sunglasses give a shaded effect. They make everything look darker and dimmer. Adding black to a colour creates the same result as putting on a pair of sunglasses; the original colour looks deeper and richer.

Do you like these yellow flowers?

Yes, I like them but they aren't very bright.

Shades

Use coloured pencils to colour each T-shirt with the indicated colour. Then colour over the coloured prints with a black pencil crayon.

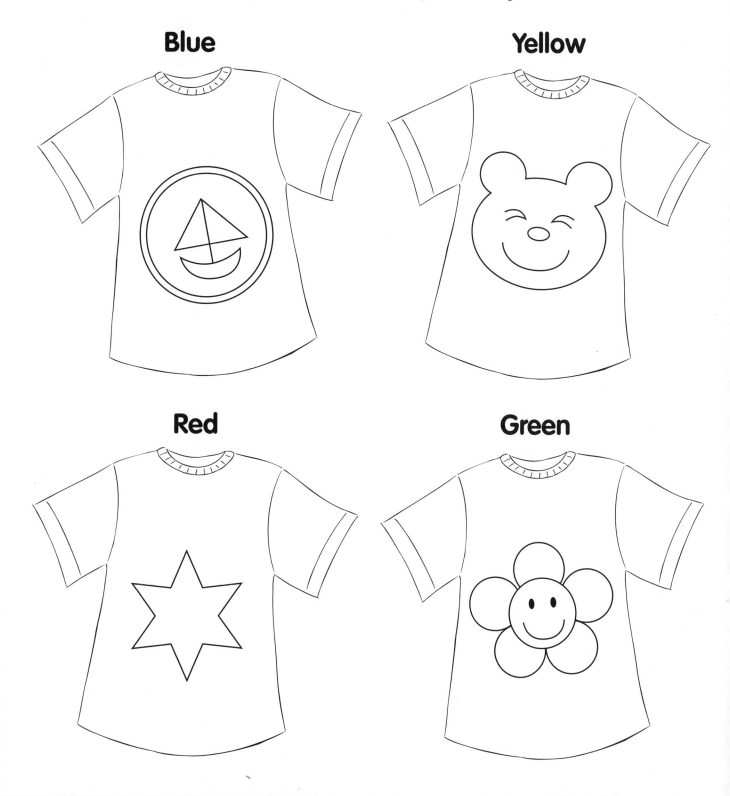

Blue

Yellow

Red

Green

Shades

Colour both cacti with a green pencil crayon. Then use a black pencil crayon and colour over the cactus on the right to show the shade.

Shades

Starry Night

Motivation:

To *experiment with mixing different colours with black*

Materials:

- grey construction paper
- red, blue, yellow, green, orange, purple, and black tempera paint
- paper plates
- paintbrushes
- white crayon
- water cans
- newspapers

What to Do:

1 Line desks with newspapers.

2 Explain to students that they are going to paint a starry night.

3 Demonstrate to students how to mix a tiny amount of black paint with other colours to create darker shades. Remind students that they need to wash their paintbrushes in water between mixing colours.

4 Tell students to think of a night scene.

5 Have students draw stars and a moon with white crayon on the construction paper.

6 Have students paint their night scene on the grey construction paper. Tell them to add black to the colours they want to use to make them look darker.

Value of a Colour

Objective: To *differentiate between the relative lightness and darkness of a colour*

Why would an artist want to mix black or white with other colours?

Imagine a world with only one tone of blue; the sky, the ocean, a blue jay, and your jeans were all in this same tone of blue. Now imagine how our world would look if the same thing happened with all the other colours!

Take a look at the things around you. Point out the different colours of red you can see. Let us look at our clothing and see which of us are wearing red. Are these reds different or similar to one another? The secret to creating these different reds is to add black or white to red.

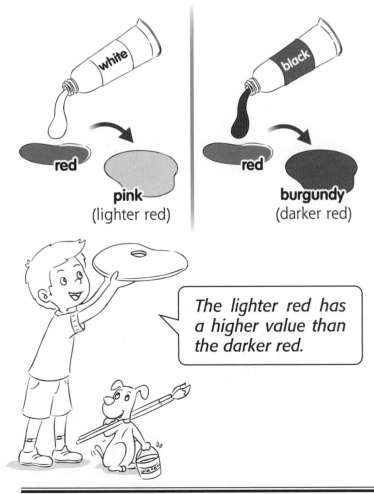

The lighter red has a higher value than the darker red.

When we describe a colour as "light" or "dark", we are talking about the **value of a colour**. The value of a colour refers to its relative lightness or darkness. White is added to make a colour lighter, while black is added to make a colour darker. To describe the value of a colour, we would say a lighter colour has a high value and a darker colour has a low value.

Value of a Colour

Colour each treat with different values of the indicated colour using paint.

> You can add black or white to get a colour in different values.

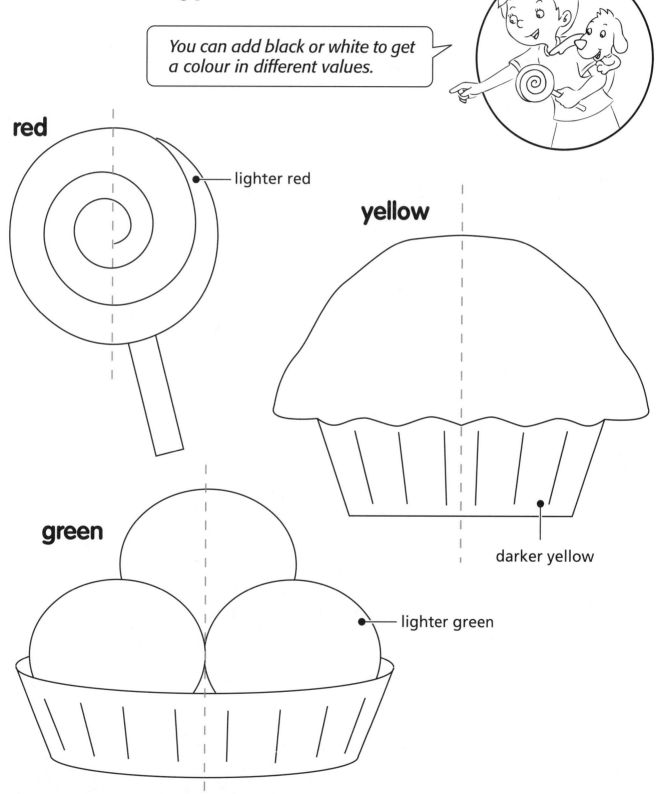

red — lighter red

yellow — darker yellow

green — lighter green

Value of a Colour

Colour each clothing item and describe the value of the colour.

T-shirt: red

pants: blue

Describe the value of a colour using the words "higher" and "lower".

Value of a Colour

Monochromatic Collages

Materials:

- old magazines
- scissors
- glue
- construction paper

Motivation:

To examine the different values of a colour

What to Do:

1 Divide students into groups.

2 Assign each group a primary or secondary colour to work with.

3 Give each group some magazines and ask them to look for different values of their assigned colour in the magazines.

4 Have each group cut out the colour samples and glue them onto the construction paper to make a collage.

Follow Up:

Have students present their collages to the class. Ask students to find the highest value and the lowest value in their collages.

Contrast

Objective: To understand the term "camouflage" and how to create contrast with colours

Let's think about animals in nature. Is it better for animals to blend into or stand out from their surroundings?

When an animal is the same colour as its natural surroundings, it is said to be **camouflaged**. Camouflage is a protective strategy used by a range of animals to guard themselves against predators and is an important skill needed for many animals to survive. The arctic hare, the chameleon, and the zebra are examples of animals that use camouflage for protection.

However, not all animals use camouflage; some animals have neon bright colours, which help them stand out from their surroundings. These bright colours give predators a signal that these animals are poisonous and are not good for eating. Some animals that have this survival skill are snakes and poisonous frogs.

When a bright colour stands out from its surrounding colours, it causes a **contrast**. Contrast is created when a high value (light) colour is paired with a low value (dark) colour.

The polar bear can blend into its surroundings. Can you find the polar bear?

Contrast

Colour the background and the objects with the indicated colours using paint. Then add white or black to create a lighter or darker value and answer the question below.

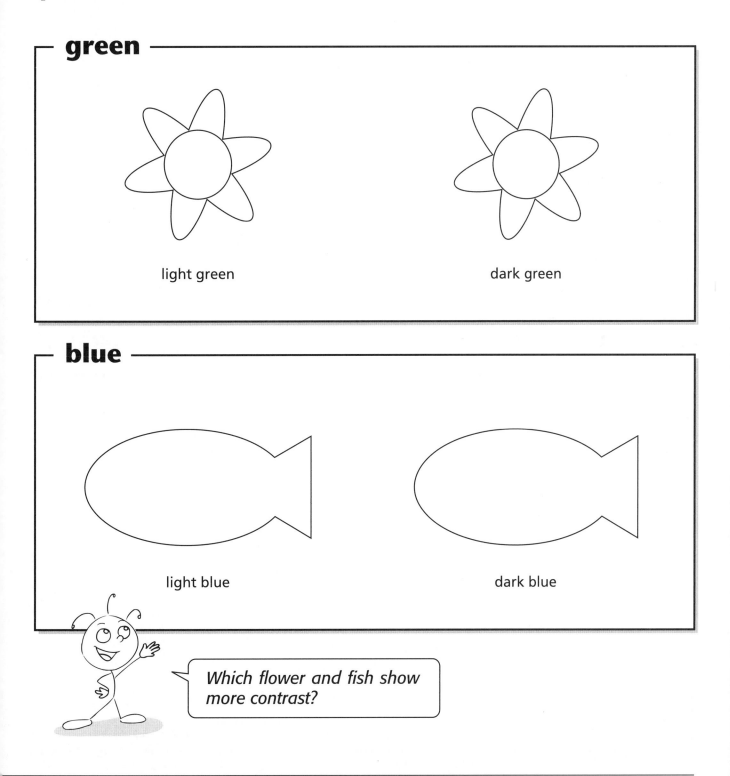

green

light green   dark green

blue

light blue   dark blue

Which flower and fish show more contrast?

Contrast

Find from old magazines two pictures of animals that live in the environments below. Cut them out and glue one of them in each box. Then colour the picture to make one show camouflage and the other contrast.

camouflage

contrast

Contrast

Be a Standout!

Motivation:

To examine how to create a contrasting effect with the use of colour

Materials:

- glue
- scissors
- white, black, and grey construction paper

What to Do:

1 Divide the class into three groups.

2 Distribute construction paper to each group.

Group 1	**Group 2**	**Group 3**
white + grey paper	**black + grey paper**	**white + black paper**

3 Have each group create their own pattern by cutting and gluing shapes onto their assigned paper.

- Group 1: glues white shapes onto the grey paper
- Group 2: glues black shapes onto the grey paper
- Group 3: glues white shapes onto the black paper

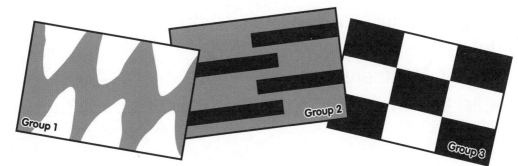

Discussion:

Discuss with students which patterns show up the most. Encourage students to use the term "contrast" in their discussion.

Colour Meanings

Objective: *To understand how specific colours can represent moods and emotions*

What colour comes to mind when you think of anger?

What colour comes to mind when you think of sadness?

What colour comes to mind when you think of happiness?

Colour is everywhere. Do you know that colours are related to **feelings** and **emotions**? Many people believe that seeing a particular colour can cause a specific emotion. For example, when seeing red, we may feel warm, excited, or tense. Good artists choose and use colours skilfully in their paintings to pass on messages to viewers.

Colours are used everywhere and appeal to our feelings without our even realizing it. Primary colours are used most often in playgrounds to stimulate our minds, while tints of colours are used most often in doctor's offices, hospitals, and nurseries to create calming and soothing environments, giving people a sense of peace.

What colour comes to mind when you think of a playground?

Name: _____   Date: _____

Colour Meanings

Colour each expression with the first colour that comes to your mind when you see it.

Colour Meanings

Be a painter. Colour the pictures with appropriate colours.

A Doctor's Office

A Playground

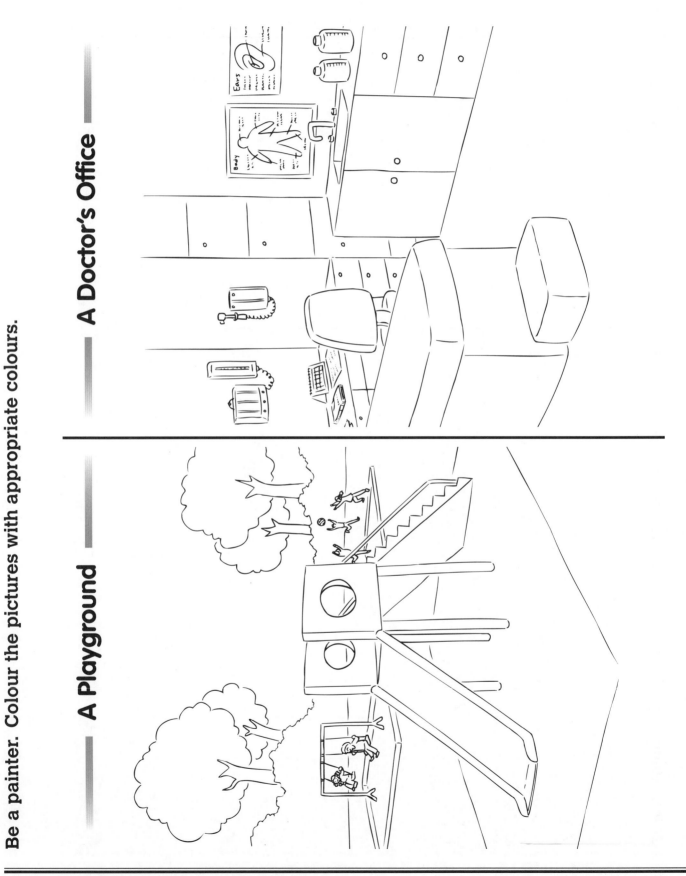

                    Art Lessons | G.1 & 2

Colour Meanings

My Colour Emotion Animal

Motivation:

To *express emotions and feelings through the use of colour*

Materials:

- pencils
- crayons
- drawing paper

What to Do:

1 Ask students to pick an animal of their choice and use a pencil to draw the animal on the drawing paper.

2 Once students have finished drawing their animals, have them choose a colour or colours to represent the specific mood that they want to convey in their drawing. For example, colour a polar bear blue or grey if they want it to be sad, or yellow or pink if they want it to be happy.

I coloured my bear yellow to show its happiness!

3 Emphasize that there is no right or wrong colour. Everyone associates his or her feelings with different colours. This activity can be used to familiarize students with expressing their emotions through art.

Follow Up:

Ask students to share their artwork with the class and talk about what emotion they were trying to convey.

The Kinds of Lines

Objective: *To learn about the different kinds of lines*

Look around the classroom and name some lines you know. Can you tell me something about the lines you've found?

If I draw two dots on the board, can you show me ways to get from one of these dots to the other?

A line has a beginning and an end. Lines can be straight, jagged, broken, or curvy.

Straight Lines

- They are predictable, since they go in one direction.
- They are the lines made by a ruler.

Jagged Lines

- They have toothed edges and resemble zigzags.
- They look like lightning bolts.

Broken Lines

- They are choppy and resemble dashes.
- They can be used to show paths that lead to a hidden treasure on a treasure map.

Curvy Lines

- They can be used to show movement in lively subjects.
- A roller coaster has a lot of curvy lines.

64   Art Lessons | G.1 & 2

The Kinds of Lines

Cut and paste the lines into their correct boxes and extend the lines to the other end of each box.

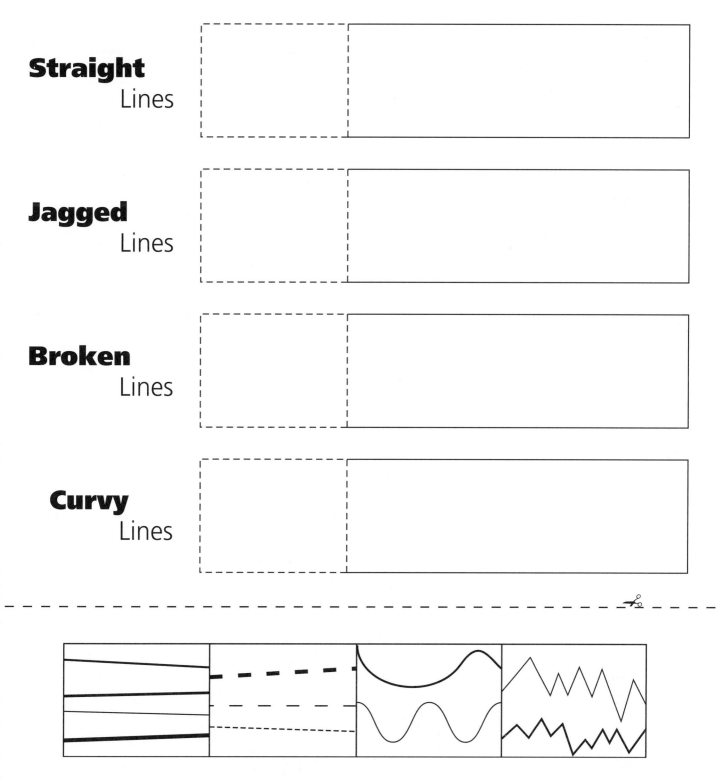

Straight Lines

Jagged Lines

Broken Lines

Curvy Lines

The Kinds of Lines

Name the appropriate lines to be used to complete the pictures. Then draw the lines.

Buildings (_____ lines)

Paths on a Map (_____ lines)

Steam (_____ lines)

Lightning (_____ lines)

       Art Lessons | G.1 & 2

The Kinds of Lines

Funky Shoe Prints

Materials:

- paper
- pencils
- crayons

Motivation:

To *apply the different kinds of lines in drawings*

What to Do:

1 Ask students to take off one of their shoes and examine the design on the sole. Notice how it is made up of different kinds of lines.

2 Have students place the shoe bottom on their paper and trace around the edge of the shoe.

3 Ask students to create their own design on their shoe prints.

4 Cut out the shoe print.

Teacher Tip:

Tape students' shoe prints on the wall and up onto the ceiling as whimsical classroom decorations.

Horizontal, Vertical, and Diagonal Lines

Objective: To distinguish the directions of lines

What do you call lines that go up and down, left to right, or corner to corner?

> Look around the classroom. Can you find lines that go in different directions?

Not only can lines be straight, jagged, broken, and curvy, they can also have different directions.

- The lines run across, from left to right, or from right to left, suggesting a feeling of rest.

- They communicate a sense of height because they go up and down.
- A skyscraper looks like a tall vertical line, standing straight up, reaching up to the sky.

- They are drawn from the top left-hand corner to the bottom right-hand corner, or vice versa.
- They grab viewers' attention. Have you ever noticed that some warning signs have diagonal lines on them?

68   Art Lessons | G.1 & 2

Horizontal, Vertical, and Diagonal Lines

Draw horizontal, vertical, or diagonal lines on the children's clothes to create a feeling of rest or interest.

Lines
horizontal – red
vertical – blue
diagonal – yellow

Horizontal, Vertical, and Diagonal Lines

Draw lines in the boxes to show the different feelings or movements indicated.

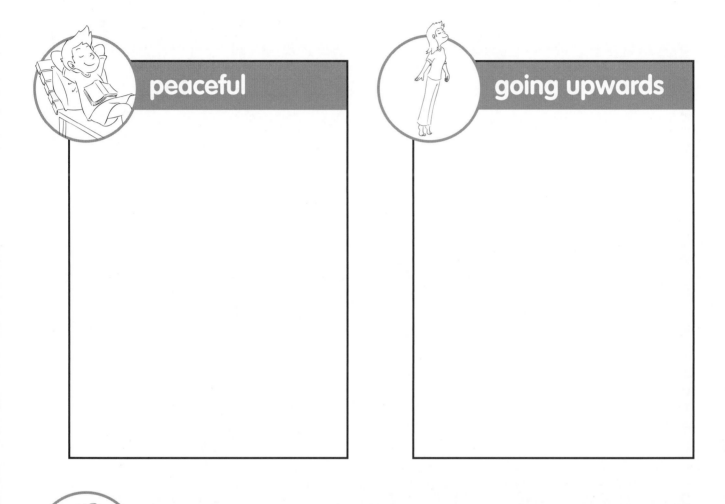

peaceful

going upwards

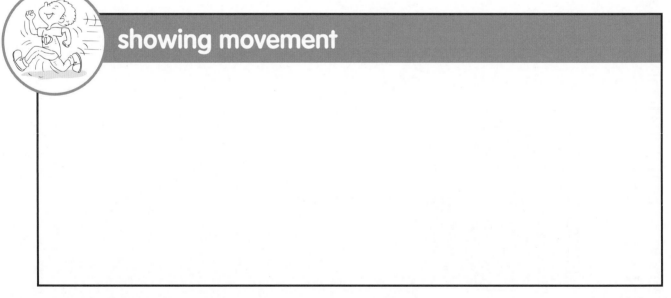

showing movement

 Art Lessons | G.1 & 2

Horizontal, Vertical, and Diagonal Lines

Fuzzy Bugs

Motivation:

To *apply knowledge of lines and patterns to create crawling, textured creatures*

Materials:

- construction paper
- yarn in assorted colours, cut in strips of 2" to 4"
- scissors
- glue
- masking tape
- pipe cleaners
- googly eyes

What to Do:

1 Cut the construction paper into a large oval shape.

2 Show students how to decorate the oval vertically, horizontally, or diagonally by gluing on the long pieces of yarn.

3 Have the students cover one side of the oval with yarn.

4 Once finished, students can glue on the googly eyes and tape pipe cleaners on the back side of the oval as arms and legs.

Geometric Shapes

Objective: *To understand that shapes are made up of lines*

What shapes can you name?

Can you point out some shapes around the classroom?

A shape is made by a line that begins and ends at the same place. There are many kinds of shapes. There are triangles, squares, rectangles, circles, and ovals. Geometric shapes have straight sides or regularly shaped curves.

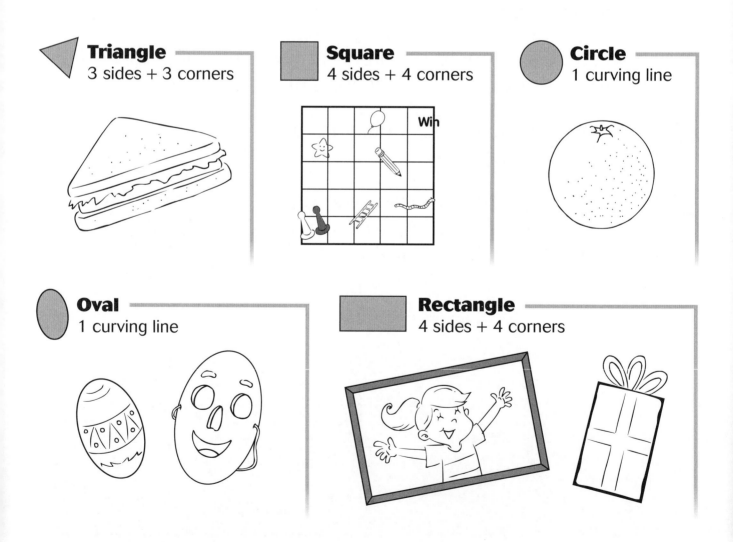

Triangle
3 sides + 3 corners

Square
4 sides + 4 corners

Circle
1 curving line

Oval
1 curving line

Rectangle
4 sides + 4 corners

Geometric Shapes

Colour the shapes with their assigned colours.

◯ : **red** ☐ : **blue** △ : **yellow**

▭ : **green** ⬭ : **orange**

Geometric Shapes

Colour the shapes and cut them out. Create images with some or all of the shapes. Then glue them onto the picture below.

Geometric Shapes

Shapes Art

Materials:

- glue
- construction paper in assorted colours
- markers

Motivation:

To *use a combination of geometric shapes to create art work*

What to Do:

1 Have students cut out some geometric shapes from the construction paper.

2 Examine the different shapes with students.

3 Brainstorm on how to arrange the shapes into a work of art. For example, a triangle can be the roof of a house.

4 Encourage your students to think about what picture they want to create, using a variety of shapes.

5 Have students glue their designs onto the construction paper and then use markers to draw in details.

Discussion:

Have students share their art work with the class. Encourage students to explain their works using proper geometric vocabulary.

Organic Shapes

Objective: To identify organic shapes in our surroundings

Imagine you are walking in a forest. What are some of the natural shapes you would see?

The shapes we find in nature are called **organic shapes**. Organic shapes occur naturally and have a curvy appearance. Some examples of organic shapes are clouds, raindrops, apples, and butterflies.

We sometimes use geometric shapes in our drawings to represent organic shapes that are found in nature. For example, we can use a circle for a cat's head, two triangles for its ears, two ovals for its eyes, and a triangle for its nose.

Organic Shapes

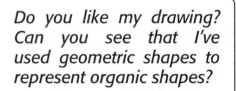

Do you like my drawing? Can you see that I've used geometric shapes to represent organic shapes?

                               Art Lessons | G.1 & 2

Organic Shapes

Colour the organic shapes.

Organic Shapes

Draw the given images again using only geometric shapes.

1.

2.

3.

   Art Lessons | G.1 & 2

Organic Shapes

Leafy Design

Motivation:

To *become familiar with the organic shapes of leaves*

Materials:

- leaves in varied shapes and sizes (5-6 per student)
- white paper
- pencils
- black markers
- crayons (orange, red, yellow, and brown)

What to Do:

1 Ask students to arrange their leaves on their paper.

2 Carefully trace around the leaves with a pencil.

3 Then go over the leaf outlines with black marker.

4 Remove the leaves and colour the spaces inside the leaf shapes with autumn colours.

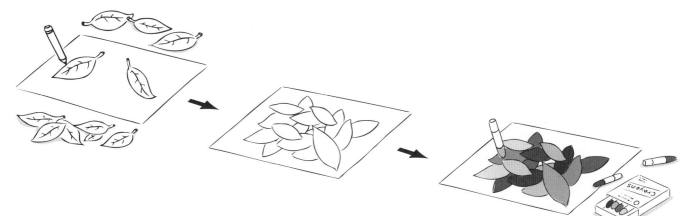

Teacher Tip:

This activity is best done in autumn. The teacher can take students outside for a stroll around the school, talk about why leaves change colour in autumn, and collect leaves together for the activity.

Symmetrical Shapes

Objective: To identify symmetrical shapes

Have you ever looked inside a kaleidoscope? What did you see?

Do you know what symmetry is?

Every new image created inside a kaleidoscope when it is turned forms a pattern that has a line of symmetry.

Symmetry occurs when a shape can be divided into two identical halves. When a shape can be folded in half and match on both sides, we call that a **symmetrical shape**.

Look at the shapes around our classroom. Can you find any shapes that can be divided into two identical halves?

Triangles, squares, rectangles, circles, and ovals are some geometric shapes that are symmetrical. Butterflies, leaves, and starfish are some organic shapes that are symmetrical.

The folded line is a line of symmetry. Do you see that it divides the shape into two identical halves?

                    Art Lessons | G.1 & 2

Symmetrical Shapes

Cut and paste the letters onto the correct spaces.

> *If you can fold the cutout to get two identical shapes, it is symmetrical.*

Symmetrical   **Not Symmetrical**

T   J   F   D

Symmetrical Shapes

Draw the missing parts to complete the symmetrical picture. Then colour it.

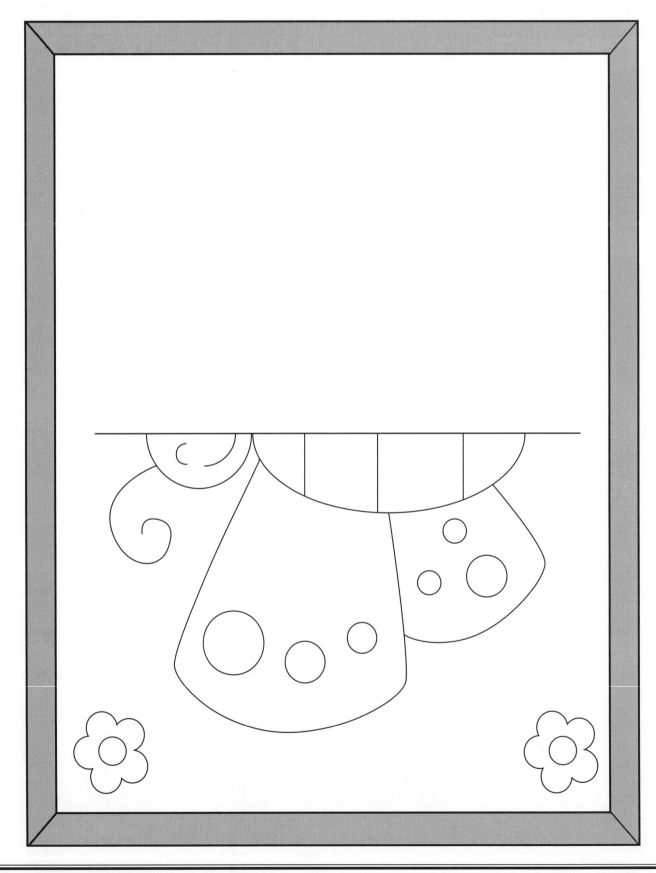

          Art Lessons | G.1 & 2

Symmetrical Shapes

I am Seeing Double!

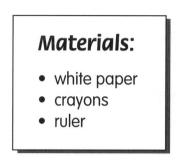

Materials:

- white paper
- crayons
- ruler

Motivation:

To *create shapes that are symmetrical*

What to Do:

1 Discuss symmetry with students and come up with a list of symmetrical objects.

2 Ask students to fold the paper in half.

3 Have students draw a simple design on one side of the paper pressing down firmly with the crayon. Emphasize that the design must be touching the folded line (line of symmetry).

4 Fold the paper in half so the design is now inside.

5 Rub over the back of the design several times with a ruler.

6 Open the paper. The design should now be faintly mirrored onto the other side of the paper.

7 Highlight the mirrored image with crayons.

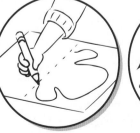

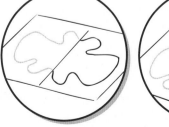

Forms

Objective: *To be able to identify the properties of forms*

Can you spot the differences between a picture of a swing and a real swing?

Can you spot the differences between a picture of a ball and a real ball?

Shapes that are flat are **two dimensional**. A picture of a ball is flat and is two dimensional. Shapes that have depth are **three dimensional**. A real ball that we can throw and bounce is three dimensional.

Have you ever read a pop-up book? How is a pop-up book different from a normal book?

The pages in a normal book are flat and are two dimensional, whereas the pages in a pop-up book pop out at you when you flip the page. The pop-up pictures make the images on the pages three dimensional.

While three-dimensional objects are called "shapes" in daily life and in mathematics, artists call three-dimensional objects **forms**.

Objects that are not flat are three dimensional. We call them forms when we study art.

Do you like my pop-up book?

We are three dimensional.

Forms

Making a Pop-up Animal Card (1)

Steps:

1 Cut out the card on the next page, following the dotted lines.

2 Draw your favourite animal in the small box and colour it.

3 Fold the card in half.

4 Cut along the two thicker lines. Then fold the picture to the front and to the back.

5 Put glue on the back of the card (outside the picture area) and paste it on a piece of paper.

6 Fold the paper in half and push out the picture.

7 The card is done!

to the front

to the back

fold

Forms

Making a Pop-up Animal Card (2)

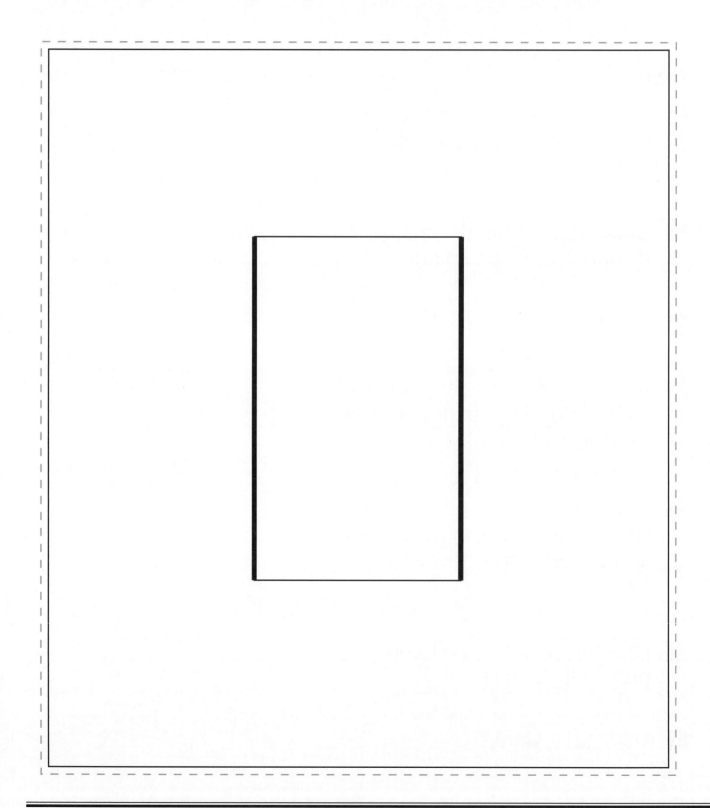

Forms

My Flower Cup

Motivation:

To turn a two-dimensional shape into a three-dimensional form

Materials:

- photocopy one worksheet per student
- standard size paper cupcake holders (2" in diameter)
- markers
- scissors
- glue

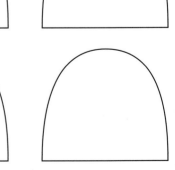

What to Do:

1 Discuss the differences between two-dimensional shapes and three-dimensional forms with students.

2 Colour the "flower" on the worksheet.

3 Cut out the petals and the head of the flower. Paste the head onto the inside bottom of the paper cupcake holder and the petals on the side of the holder.

- ✂ - - - - - - - - -

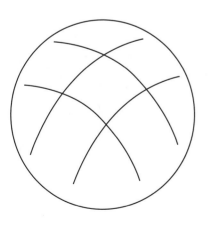

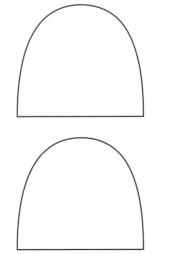

Textures

Objective: To identify and describe a variety of textures

It's soft and smooth.

Touch a piece of tissue paper and then a piece of sandpaper. How does each feel?

Texture refers to the surface quality of an object. It is how an object feels when we touch it.

When we feel an object's texture with our fingertips, we are using our **sense of touch**. The skin on our fingertips is very sensitive; it allows us to tell the difference between rough and smooth, soft and hard, and wet and dry. People who are blind can use their fingertips to read Braille by touching and feeling the patterns of raised dots on paper.

Let's brainstorm on some words that are used to describe different textures.

What material can we use to create these textures in art?

We can use a variety of objects to create textures. For example, we can use feathers for fluffy texture, burlaps for rough texture, cotton balls for soft texture, sand for grainy texture, ribbons for silky texture, and yarn for fuzzy texture.

Textures

Colour the items that have the specified texture in each group.

1. Soft

2. Rough

3. Hard

4. Smooth

Textures

Find pictures that have the textures indicated from magazines.

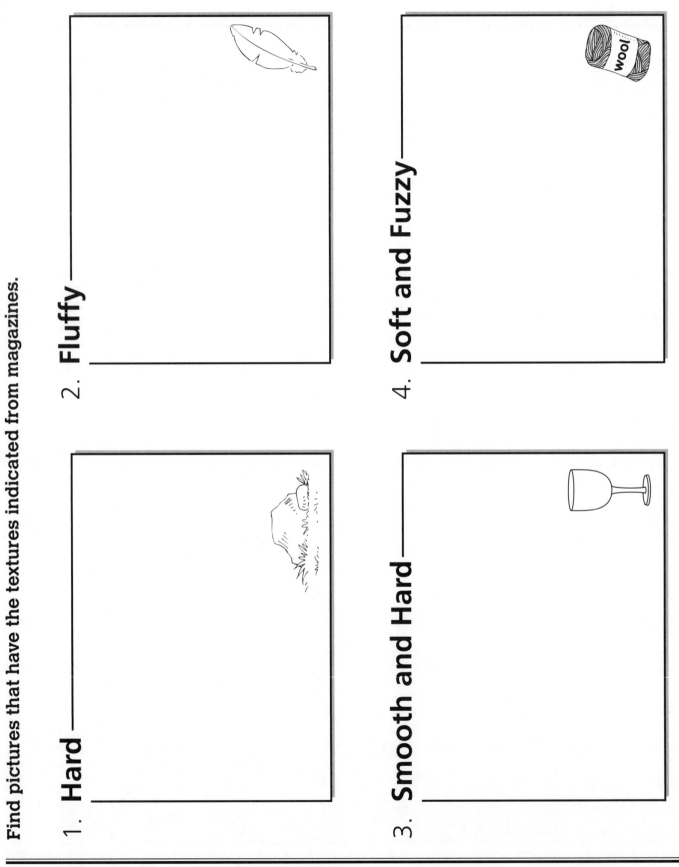

1. Hard

2. Fluffy

3. Smooth and Hard

4. Soft and Fuzzy

Textures

Landscape Mural

Motivation:

To create a textured art work by using a variety of materials

Materials:

- white or beige construction paper
- crayons, markers, or pencil crayons
- scissors
- white glue
- found materials

> Found materials include coloured paper, sandpaper, tissue paper, coloured shredded paper, cotton balls, foam, foil, buttons, yarn, feathers, etc.

What to Do:

1 Explain to students that they will be making a landscape picture with sky, clouds, grass, and any other natural objects. When they are finished, their pictures will be combined to make a mural.

2 Start by working on the sky. Students should colour the sky and then glue cotton balls on as clouds.

3 Then work on the grass. Students can choose their own materials to represent the grass.

4 Students can then work freely on any other objects they want to include in their landscape picture.

5 Once finished, the art works can be taped onto the walls as a long mural that runs around the room.

Printmaking

Objective: *To understand the concept of printmaking*

Who has used a stamp before?

What did it look like and how did you use it?

Have you ever received a stamp on your homework? Teachers often use different stamps with a variety of coloured ink pads to stamp out those cute pictures onto your work to let you know you did well. Artists sometimes use tools similar to stamps to create a specific kind of art. The use of these stamp-like tools is an art technique called printmaking.

Printmaking is the process of creating an image on a flat surface like rubber, rock, or wood, and transferring that image onto another surface like a piece of paper or cloth.

To create a print, we first have to carve or engrave an image onto a flat surface. In the old days, people made engravings on rocks or carved images in wood. Nowadays, we can use softer materials such as rubber and Styrofoam to make the carving process easier. Once we have created the carved image, we can dab some paint onto it and transfer the image onto paper.

Wow! That's a big stamp.

Printmaking

Cut out and glue the correct prints next to their matching stamps.

Printmaking

See how Emma created a picture using a stamp. Design your own picture and create it using stamps.

I created my lovely apple with a panda stamp.

Printmaking

It's a Stampede!

Motivation:

To create a Styrofoam stamp with a central theme and produce a print from it

Materials:

- Styrofoam plates
- cardboard
- tempera paint
- roller or paintbrush
- pencils
- scissors
- glue
- paper

What to Do:

1 Choose a theme and ask students to think of an image within the theme that they would like to make a print of.

2 Students should then sketch out the image they want for their stamp. The image should be solid so that it can be cut out easily.

3 Students should then get a Styrofoam plate and draw their themed image on the Styrofoam plate with a pencil.

4 Once the drawing is complete, students can cut the image out.

5 Glue the image onto a piece of cardboard and let it dry.

6 Lightly roll the tempera paint over the Styrofoam image, trying not to get paint onto the cardboard.

7 Press a piece of paper onto the Styrofoam image.

8 Carefully remove the paper from the image.

Self Portraits

Objective: To examine facial features to create a self portrait

Close your eyes and use your hands to feel your face. Start at your forehead and work your way down to your chin. How does your face feel?

A **self portrait** is a representation of an artist done by the artist himself or herself. A self portrait can be a painting, a photograph, or a sculpture. A self portrait not only shows the face, but can also suggest or reveal the personality, interests, and lifestyle of the artist.

We can use a mirror to help us draw a self portrait. To begin, take a good look at your face; study the shape of your eyes, nose, and mouth. Then notice where each facial feature is located. Our eyes are about midway between the top of our head and the bottom of our chin. The two sides of our face should be somewhat symmetrical. We should always use curvy lines to draw since the face is smooth and soft.

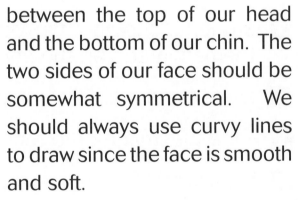

Annie, do you think my self portrait is cute?

Self Portraits

Check the pictures that are self portraits.

Self Portraits

Identify the features of your face by checking the correct boxes. Glue a close-up picture of yourself in the circle. Then draw a self portrait.

Face

Eyes

Mouth

Nose

My Self Portrait

         Art Lessons | G.1 & 2

Self Portraits

This Is Me!

Motivation:

To *create a simple yet expressive self portrait*

Materials:

- a photo of each student enlarged in black and white on blank paper (use students' school photos)
- overhead acetates
- overhead markers
- wet paper towels
- tape

What to Do:

1 Print a 8 x 10" photo of each student using a black and white printer.

2 Provide each student with a sheet of overhead acetate and each table group with a box of overhead markers.

3 Tape the photo on the bottom or rough side of the overhead acetate.

4 Demonstrate to students how to trace the features of their face on the acetate and how to wipe the marker off the acetate using wet paper towels.

5 Students then trace over their photos with markers.

6 Once finished, let the students guess whose self portraits are drawn on the acetates. Then tape the acetate portraits on the classroom windows.

Is this you, Teddy?

Rock Sculptures

Objective: *To appreciate and be familiar with rock sculptures*

Who knows what rock sculptures are? Can anyone give an example of a rock sculpture?

There are many rock sculptures in the world. Here is an example: an **inuksuk** is a mysterious human-made stone landmark found throughout the Arctic region. It is a stack of rocks balanced on each other, forming a human-like figure.

Where else can we find sculptures made of rocks?

Mount Rushmore is a famous tourist attraction in South Dakota, United States. It is a giant sculpture of the heads of four former United States presidents on the side of a mountain. It is an impressive rock sculpture that took 14 years to complete!

The **Great Sphinx** in Egypt is the largest rock sculpture ever made by man. The Sphinx has the head of a human and the body of a lion. It is believed that the Sphinx was the guardian of the Egyptians' tombs and temples.

Nowadays, rock sculptures can be a form of art that people can display in their homes. Rock sculptures are often used as garden or pond decorations.

100   Art Lessons | G.1 & 2

Rock Sculptures

Cut out the sculptures. Then glue them into the correct boxes.

Taj Mahal
a big palace

Ahu Akivi
mysterious figures

The Great Wall
a giant wall

Mount Rushmore
famous faces

India

U.S.A.

China

Easter Island

Rock Sculptures

Check the circle if the sculpture is made of rock; otherwise, put a cross.

Rock Sculptures

We Rock!

Materials:

- rocks of various sizes and shapes

Motivation:

To *examine how balance and stability are achieved in a three-dimensional sculpture*

What to Do:

1 Divide the class into groups of four or five.

2 Provide each group with many rocks of various sizes.

3 Have each group make a rock sculpture by stacking rocks on top of each other.

Use bigger rocks on the bottom. Pay attention to how the rocks balance.

4 Once finished, students can share their rock sculptures with the class. Take a photo of each rock sculpture before letting students tear it down.

Discussion:

Discuss with students how they made their rock sculptures and the tricks and tips they discovered in building them. Ask what made the sculptures strong and stable.

Elements of Design

Objective: *To identify and describe the elements of design in a work of art*

How do we describe a work of art?

What words would you use to describe a piece of art?

To describe a work of art, we need to be familiar with the elements of design in art. The elements of design include colours, lines, shapes, forms, and textures of an artwork and how they make us feel.

Let's review some elements of design that we have learned this year.

 **Colour**

What kind of colours do you see?

Are they bright, light, or dark?

Are they tints or shades?

 **Line**

Are the lines straight, jagged, broken, or curvy?

Are they horizontal, vertical, or diagonal?

 **Shape and Form**

Can you see any shapes or forms in the artwork?

Are they geometric, organic, or symmetrical?

 **Texture**

Are there any textures?

Are they rough, smooth, dry, or wet?

 **Mood**

How does the work make you feel?

What do you think the artist is trying to say in this art piece?

Elements of Design

Colour the pictures and trace the lines as instructed. Then answer the questions.

1. Colour the flower red and yellow. Trace the dotted lines with a green marker.

2. Colour the flower purple and blue. Trace and thicken the dotted lines with a brown marker.

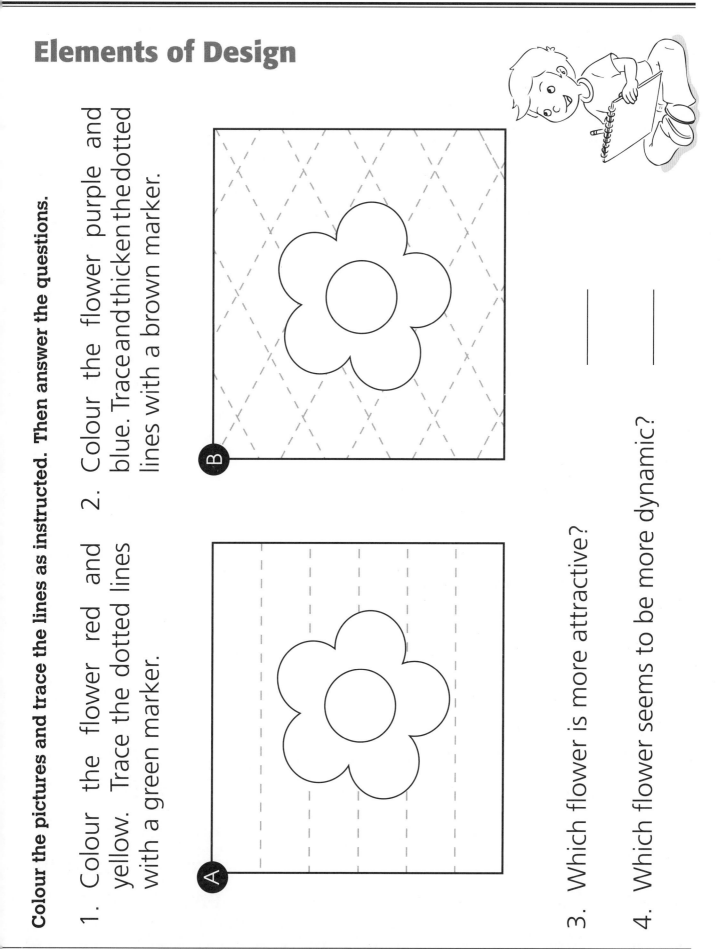

3. Which flower is more attractive? _____

4. Which flower seems to be more dynamic? _____

Elements of Design

Make your name into a piece of art, using colours, lines, shapes and textures to suggest a mood. Then ask a classmate to describe your work.

Artist:

Elements of Design

described by

Colours

| bright | dark |
| light | heavy |

Shapes

geometric   organic   symmetrical

Lines

thick	thin
straight	jagged
broken	curvy

Textures

smooth	bumpy
fuzzy	fluffy
hard	soft

Mood

happy	sad
excited	peaceful
angry	cold

Elements of Design

Artistic Elements

Materials:

- students' art portfolio
- lined paper
- drawing paper
- pencils and erasers
- pencil crayons

Motivation:

To *describe the artistic elements that are present in an artwork and create a piece of art that matches a specific description*

What to Do:

1 Ask each student to pick a work of art from his or her portfolio.

2 Give students a model of how to write a description of their work. Tell them to pay attention to colours, lines, shapes and forms, textures, and mood.

Description:
- a flower in an organic shape
- bright colours
- makes you feel happy

Ann

Ann, I followed your description to draw this picture. May I see yours now?

Yes, Jonathan!

3 Ask each student to write a description of his or her work.

4 Once students are done, have them exchange their descriptions with a partner.

5 The partner reads the description through and draws a picture that matches the description.

6 Each student then compares the picture that he or she drew to the original work that was described.

Art Media

Objective: *To describe different ways in which a variety of art materials, tools, and techniques can be used*

What kind of tools and materials are needed for certain techniques?

What kind of art work do certain techniques produce?

Let's review some art techniques we have used this year.

Techniques	**Tools and Materials**
 **Printmaking**	• sponge, Styrofoam, or cardboard used as a stamp • scissors and glue to create the stencil • paper to transfer the image onto
 **Painting and Drawing**	• paint applied with a paintbrush to create images • crayons, markers, or pencil crayons used to draw images
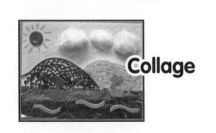 **Collage**	• construction paper, feathers, ribbons, buttons, beads, yarn, cloth, and other found materials to create interesting textures • scissors and glue to hold the materials in place
 **Construction**	• clay, play dough, stones, wire, etc. to create a sculpture

Art Media

Colour the materials used in each art technique.

1. Printmaking

2. Painting and Drawing

3. Collage

4. Construction

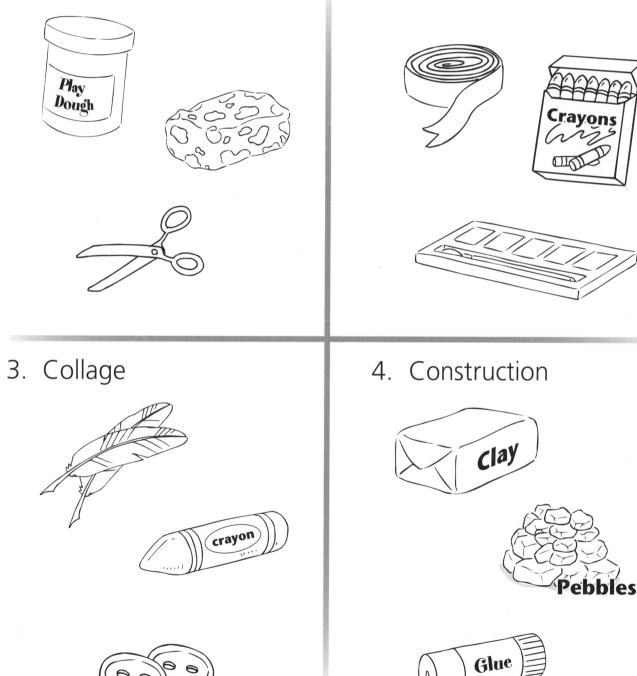

Art Media

Cut out the materials or tools the children need to complete their work and paste them next to the correct descriptions.

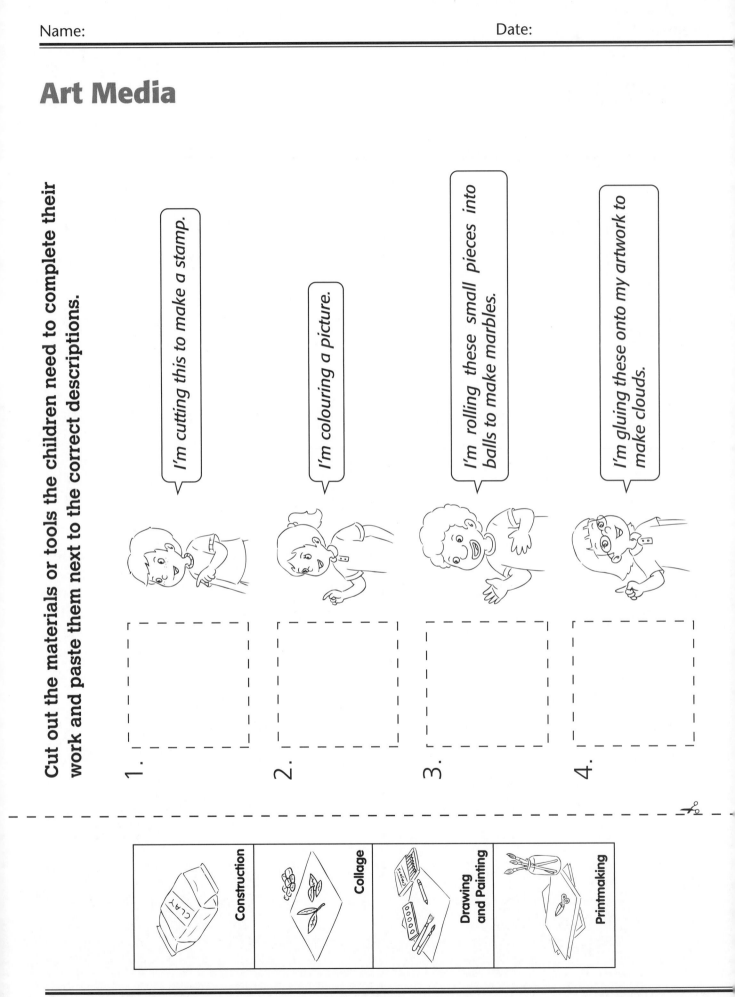

I'm cutting this to make a stamp.

I'm colouring a picture.

I'm rolling these small pieces into balls to make marbles.

I'm gluing these onto my artwork to make clouds.

1.

2.

3.

4.

Construction

Collage

Drawing and Painting

Printmaking

Art Media

Artsy Brainstorming

Materials:
- chart paper
- markers

Motivation:

To illustrate different ways in which a variety of art materials and tools can be used to create a work of art

Let's think back to the various art projects we've done in this school year.

What to Do:

1 Divide students into four groups.

2 Assign one art technique per group.

3 Ask students to discuss their art technique among their group. Ask them to think about what tools or materials the technique uses, and what effects can be achieved by applying that art technique.

4 Put down their ideas on the chart paper. For example, with printmaking, students can draw stamps, stencils, and a picture of what printmaking artwork looks like.

5 Have each group present and explain their ideas to the class.

6 At the end of each presentation, ask the rest of the class for additional ideas that can be added to each sheet of chart paper.

7 Post the chart paper on the classroom bulletin board.

Planning and Critiquing

Objective: *To learn the importance of planning an art work and to identify strengths and areas for improvement in art works*

What is the purpose of planning the creation of an art work?

When we make plans to create a piece of art, we need to think about what the art work will be about. Then we need to consider the subject of the art work. Lastly, we should think about the materials needed to create this piece of art and what techniques will be used.

What is art critique?

Art critique allows us to better understand works of art and identify the strengths and areas for improvement in our own or others' art works. The four key components in art critique are: **describe**, **analyze**, **interpret**, and **decide**.

First we describe the art work. Is it a painting, a sculpture, or a print? Then we need to analyze the art work by considering the colour, shapes, forms, textures, etc. Next, we try to interpret what the artist is trying to communicate through the art work and whether or not he or she is successful in doing it. Finally, we decide and explain whether we like the art work or not.

When we critique others' works, we provide supportive and useful feedback for the artists to recognize how they can enhance their works without hurting their feelings.

How do you think this drawing would look if it were done in watercolour paint instead?

Planning and Critiquing

Read each plan below. Cut out the art work and glue it next to the correct description.

1.

My Plan

- a picture of geometric shapes
- foam sheets and scissors
- paint and paintbrushes
- a lid for tracing

2.

My Plan

- a mobile
- wire and strings
- cardboard
- aluminum foil

3.

My Plan

- a collage
- cardboard
- paint and paintbrushes
- scissors and glue

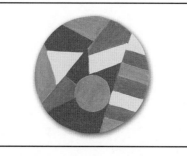

Planning and Critiquing

Find a piece of art from a magazine or newspaper. Cut and paste the picture in the box below. Then critique the art work by answering the questions.

Art Work

- What is the subject of the art work? _____

- What's one element of design used? _____

- What is the artist trying to say? _____

- Do you like the art work? Why or why not? _____

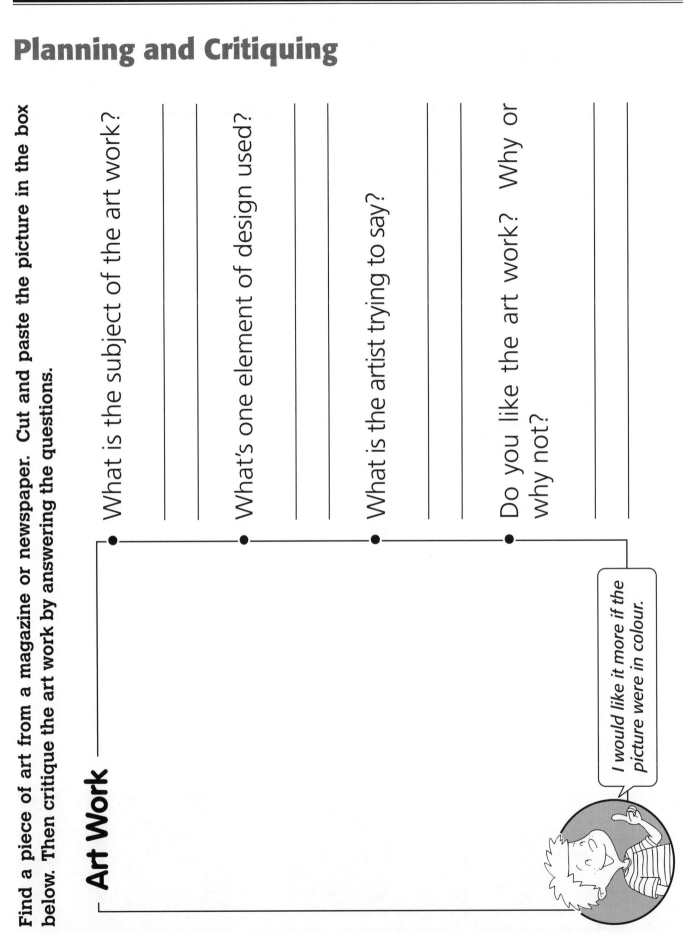

I would like it more if the picture were in colour.

114 Art Lessons | G.1 & 2

Planning and Critiquing

The Art of Critique

Materials:

- students' art portfolios
- lined paper
- pencils and erasers

Motivation:

To identify and explain strengths and areas for improvement in an art work

What to Do:

1 Ask each student to pick an art work from his or her portfolio.

2 Talk about the importance of constructive critique and encouragement with the class.

3 Explain to students that they are going to critique their own art works. Once they are done, they can choose a partner and critique each other's work.

4 Have the students model an art critique using the guidelines below.

Four Steps to Critique an Art Work:

Describe
What do you see?
What word would you use to describe this art work?

Analyze
How do you think the artist made this work?
What element of design were used in this art work?

Interpret
What do you think this art work is about?
What title would you give this painting?

Evaluate
What do you like about this art work?
What don't you like about it?

Drama
and
Dance

Drama Words

Objective: *To identify and correctly use drama vocabulary*

You can tell your neighbour all about your new bike, but if you show it to him, he or she will know exactly what you mean.

Drama has the same effect. If a story is "acted out", it becomes real and clear to us. We might think about a story or remember it more if it is acted out for us.

We can speak to others through drama, by pretending we are a **character** in a story. To do this, we need to speak, move, and respond like him or her.

I'll saddle up my horse and ride through the wild, wild West!

Out of role   **In role**

When we step out of our shoes and into the shoes of another person, pretending to be him or her, we are "in role". We are "out of role" when we step out of those shoes and are ourselves again.

When we pretend to be a character in a story, it is easier to understand how that character feels and be able to help solve problems than if we simply read the story.

Drama Words

Look at the pictures. If Simon is himself, write "out of role" below. If he is playing a character, write "in role", and guess what character he is pretending to be.

Drama Words

Help Jason and Emma get "in role." Cut them and their costumes out. Glue the astronaut outfit to one of them, and the knight outfit to the other. Then create a story about one of them.

Emma is a/an _____.

Jason is a/an _____.

Drama Words

Not My Shoes

Motivation:

To recognize and demonstrate movement sequences found in the student's natural surroundings

Materials:

- a book that shows natural change (*The Very Hungry Caterpillar* by Eric Carle)
- instrumental music
- some acorns

What to Do:

A Butterfly

Using the suggested book, talk to the students about a butterfly's life cycle. Play the music and help them imagine a butterfly's movement. Then have them pretend to be a little egg transforming into a long, slow caterpillar, to a still chrysalis, and to a big, beautiful butterfly.

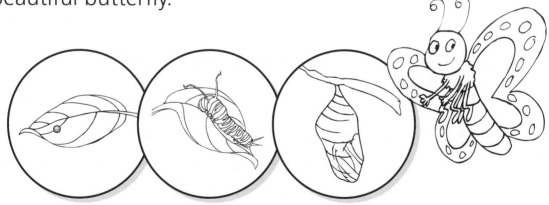

An Oak Tree

Ask the students to compare the acorns to the big, old trees they see outside. Pass the acorns around. Then have them start as a tiny acorn and transform into a tall oak tree swaying in the wind. Remind them to imagine what it would be like to be an oak tree, not just to move like one.

Speaking Out

Objective: To *identify ways in which the voice can be used to convey thoughts and feelings when playing a role*

"I will..."

How many different ways can you say these words? When answering your teacher, these words are polite. When your mom asks, "Who will go for ice cream with me?" and you answer, "I will!", your words will surely be more excited.

What kind of voice would you use if Lara's pet is a kitten? What if it is a skunk, or a lion?

We can use our voices in different ways. We can make them lower, higher, softer, or louder. We can use different voices to show emotions like joy, sadness, surprise, fear, or anger. How would you say "Stop" if:

• your brother is bugging you?
• your dad is tickling you?
• your cat is reaching its paw into the fish bowl?

If we are acting out a character, we can make him or her more believable by changing our voice and using words that he or she would use instead of our own.

Speaking Out

How we use our voices is often connected to how we – or our characters – are feeling. How would the character in each picture say "Stop"? Choose an emotion and colour the loudness bar to show how loud you think his or her voice should be.

Emotions

joy   sadness   surprise   fear   anger   excitement

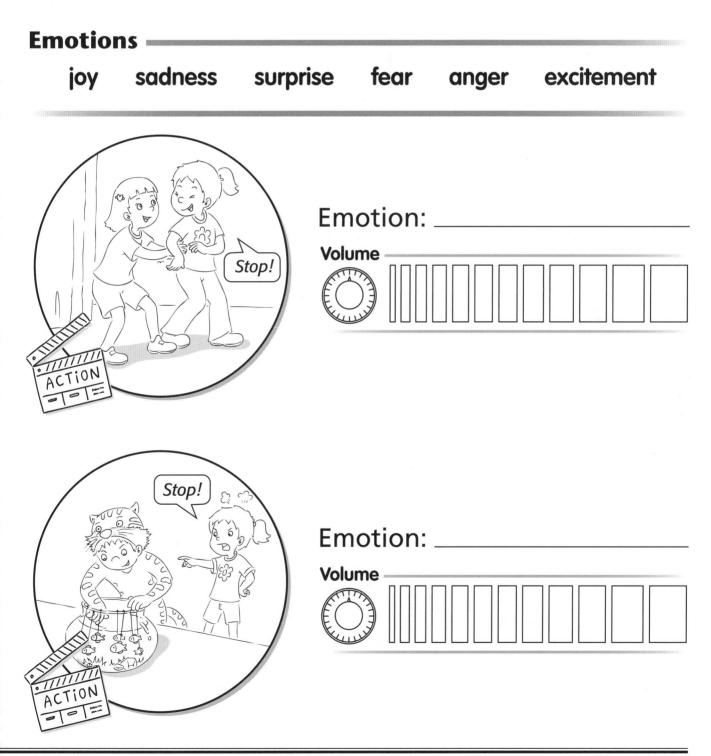

Emotion: _____

Volume

Emotion: _____

Volume

Speaking Out

Cut out the words below and decide if they belong to the lion or the mouse. Glue them into the correct boxes. Try acting like a lion or a mouse by speaking the words with different voices.

I can squeeze through the smallest hole in a wall.	I will go hunting tonight!
I would like some cheese.	I climb trees to see my prey.

rOAR!	quite quiet	Very loud!
squeak…	low voice	high voice

Speaking Out

Paper Bag Puppets

Materials:

- paper lunch bags
- large googly eyes
- markers
- felt, yarn, construction paper, etc.
- scissors
- glue

Motivation:

To *use the vocabulary and tone of voice appropriate for a specific character when playing a role*

Though most students may find acting in front of an audience intimidating, they usually feel much less inhibited as the voice of a puppet.

What to Do:

1 Have the students put on a puppet show of a story you have read in class. *The Three Little Pigs*, *Little Red Riding Hood*, or *Goldilocks* work well. Have them each choose a character.

2 Show the students how to make a basic paper bag puppet so that they understand where the eyes, nose, and mouth go.

3 Encourage them to cut out construction paper pieces to make ears, arms, etc. Use yarn for hair or fur. The more elaborate the puppets, the better.

4 Have the students practise the different voices their characters might make. What does a little pig sound like? What about a big, bad wolf?

5 Either by using a simple script or having them improvise, allow the students present their puppet plays to the class.

Magnificent Movements

Objective: To describe some basic ways in which the body can be used in space and time, and explore the variety of movements of which each body part is capable

Can you stretch your arms up and out, as if you are waking from a nap?

Can you crouch down low and slither like a snake?

There are many ways we can move our bodies. We can reach up high, like a skyscraper or squish ourselves small, like an ant. We can move as slow as a turtle or sprint across the ground like a rabbit.

We can easily make shapes with straight lines. We can make a "V" with our outstretched arms or a triangle with our body bent over. We can bend our spines and twist our muscles to make other curved shapes, too.

We can move in the space around us, making different shapes with the different parts of our bodies. What shape can you make with your knees, waist, or elbows when you reach up high or crouch down low? How much space can you take up? How small can you be?

Magnificent Movements

Look at the pictures. Decide how the children are moving and name their movements.

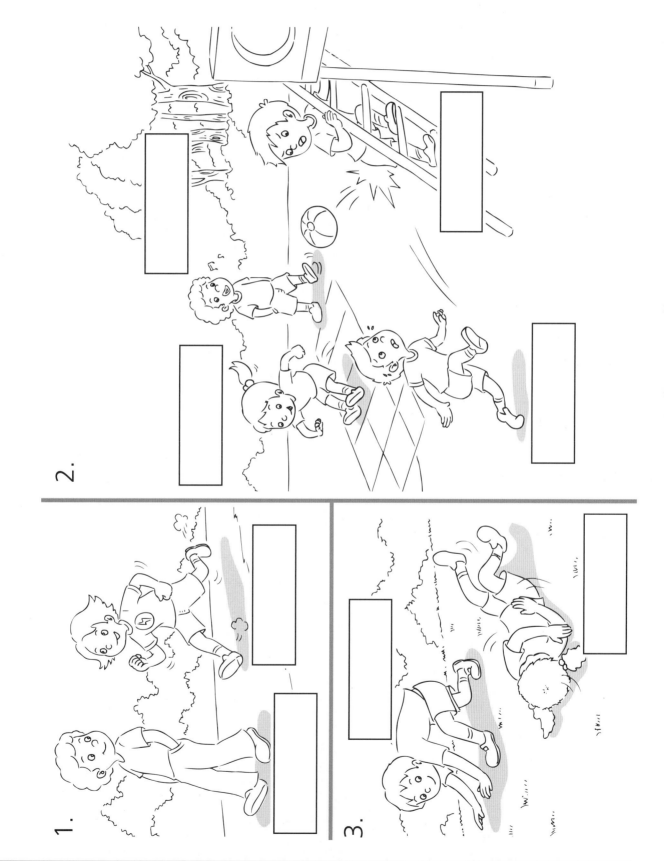

Magnificent Movements

Cut out the pictures below. Put them in the proper order to create your own sequence of movement. Then try out the movements yourself and teach your classmates.

My Movements

Steps

1

2

3

4

5

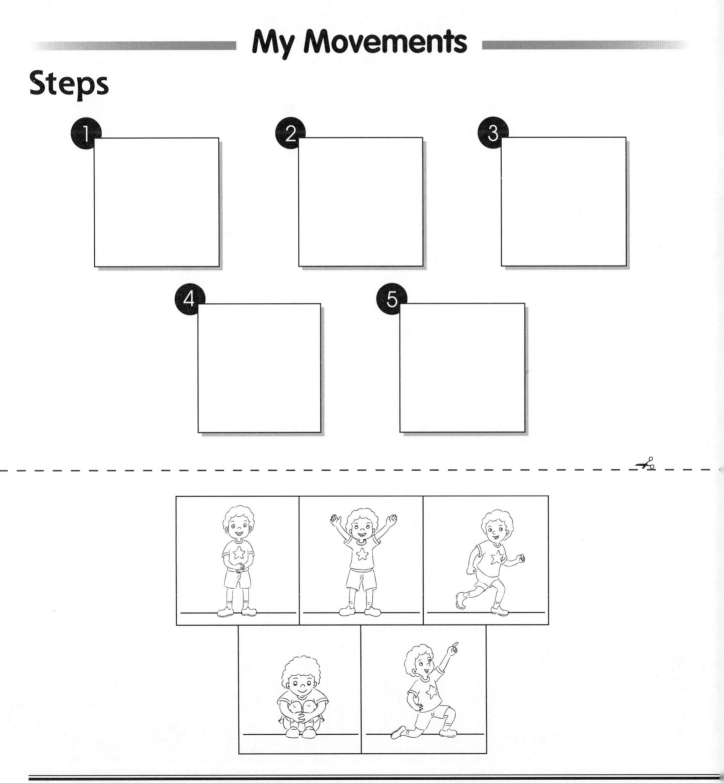

Magnificent Movements

Bear Hunt

Motivation:

To demonstrate control of one's body when moving like different animals and to recognize and demonstrate movement sequences used by specific characters or found in one's natural surroundings

Materials:

- an open area
- *We're Going on a Bear Hunt* by Michael Rosen
- music (optional)

What to Do:

1 Encourage the students to make straight or curvy lines with their bodies to create different shapes. They can partner up to create the letters of the alphabet.

2 Have the students explore the space around them by moving as though they were lions, monkeys, turtles, kangaroos, or cheetahs. Encourage one student to move like an animal, and see if the others can join his or her "pack".

3 Introduce the idea of freezing the body in one position. Encourage them to make all movements count so that when frozen, their poses are interesting and leave no doubt as to what they are.

4 Read *We're Going on a Bear Hunt* together. Ask the students to think of ways to use their bodies differently to act out this story. How can they show thick, oozing mud, a dark cave, or a forest? Have them use their bodies to re-enact the story.

Symbols

Objective: *To identify symbols relevant to the meaning of stories and poems*

What do you think of when you see this shape?

Think about the shape and what it means. A heart is a **symbol** for love.   On Valentine's Day, you see hearts everywhere!

We use other symbols to stand for holidays. A candy cane, lit tree, or snowflake may remind us of Christmas. A picture of a turkey may make Thanksgiving come to mind. What holidays do you think of when you see a bunny or a Jack o'lantern?

The maple leaf, loon, and beaver are all symbols of our country. When we sing *O Canada*, we look at a symbol of our pride: the Canadian flag.

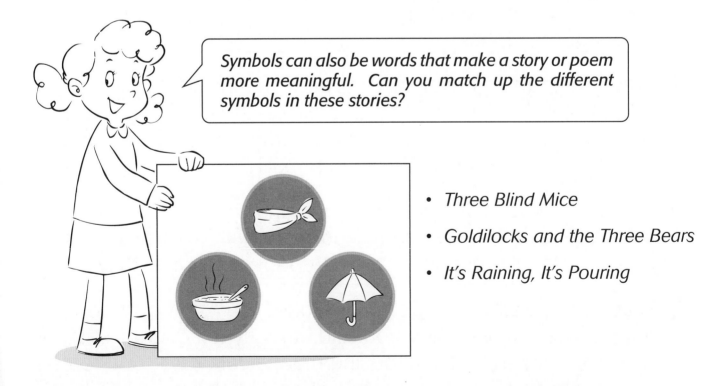

Symbols can also be words that make a story or poem more meaningful. Can you match up the different symbols in these stories?

- *Three Blind Mice*
- *Goldilocks and the Three Bears*
- *It's Raining, It's Pouring*

Symbols

Do you know what the images below symbolize? Write your answers on the lines. Then draw one more symbol and see if your classmates know what it symbolizes.

1.

2.

3.

4.

5.

6.

7.

It symbolizes...

_____ .

Symbols

- **The Ant and the Grasshopper**
- **Goldilocks and the Three Bears**
- **The Tortoise and the Hare**

Think about the symbols that can be found in the stories mentioned below. Then cut out the pictures and match them to the messages they symbolize by gluing them in the spaces provided.

It is wrong to take what is not yours.

Slow and steady wins the race.

If you work hard when things are easy, you will be rewarded when things get harder.

If you're really fast but take breaks too often, you may not win the race.

✂ ─ ─ ─ ─ ─ ─ ─ ─ ─ ─ ─ ─ ─ ─ ─ ─ ─

Symbols

Creative Fables

Materials:

- pictures of simple symbols (hearts, stars, trees, etc.)
- paper (optional)
- crayons, markers, pencil crayons (optional)

Motivation:

To *understand symbols and use one's imagination to think of stories that use specific symbols*

What to Do:

1 Show the class the symbols you have chosen. Ask them what they think each one symbolizes.

2 Once everyone has come up with ideas, divide the students into groups of two or three, and give each group a symbol.

My story is about a small heart becoming big.

3 Ask each group to come up with a story that features the symbol as a character, a setting, or an object. The story does not have to be long or complicated. Just a short fable will do. It might help to remind the students of stories like *The Vain Crow (cheese)*, *The Fox and the Grapes (grapes)*, or *A Mother's Love (heart)*.

4 Ask each group to tell the class their story – with pictures they have drawn if time permits.

5 Discuss with the whole class how each group's symbol works in each story.

In a Role

Objective: *To speak in role as characters in a story, assuming the attitude and gestures of the people they are playing*

Think of your favourite movie.

It has people in it called actors and actresses, playing different roles. These actors and actresses show different feelings on their faces and talk in special ways so that you will believe that they are the characters in the story.

A character in a story can be:

nice, gentle, happy, mean, brave, lonely, messy, friendly

How could you show these character traits in the way you speak or move?

frightened   scary

Let's say you are going to play the character of the big, bad wolf in *Three Little Pigs*. Since you are not a wolf, you have to use your imagination and pretend that you are. How would the wolf "talk"? Would he have a high, squeaky voice, or a low, loud growl? How would he move? How would you show that he is up to trouble, even before he speaks?

We can better understand poems and stories by seeing them acted out. We can even see our own difficult situations solved more easily by "role playing", or pretending to be others.

In a Role

The students are putting on a play. Cut out the lines below and glue them onto the correct speech bubbles.

Leave us alone. We're not interested in the fur you're selling.

Can you help me find the bus station?

Please, officers, my friend and I need your help.

Of course we can help. What is the problem?

In a Role

A. Describe the expression on each character's face.

angry   happy   caring   sad   bored   sleepy

1. _____

2. _____

3. _____

4. _____

5. _____

6. _____

B. Find a picture of a person with an interesting expression on his or her face. Cut it out and glue it in the space provided. Then describe his or her expression.

His/Her Expression:

_____

In a Role

Masquerade Masks

Materials:

- Bristol board – cut into basic partial mask shape (eyes cut out, and hole punched on sides)
- elastic string
- tempera paint, paint brushes, and glue
- feathers, tissue, and construction paper
- sequins, beads, foil, ribbons, etc.
- *Henny Penny* or *The Little Red Hen*

Motivation:

To *play different characters using voice, expression, gestures, and a mask to help free the imagination*

What to Do:

1 Read *Henny Penny* or *The Little Red Hen* with the students. Talk about the different characters and how they would speak or move.

2 After showing examples of some masks, have the students decorate their own masks. Position feathers in a fan, away from the centre of the mask and out to make a bird. A triangular piece of construction paper or Bristol board can be folded and secured outwards from the mask to make a beak. Tissue paper, already cut in teardrop shapes, can be applied in the same way to make fur, feathers, etc. Extend decorations beyond the mask for a more realistic effect.

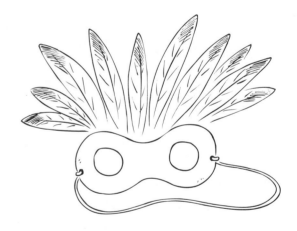

3 Have the students explore the voice and movements of their characters. Take time to practise playing "in role" before acting out the story.

Real Movements

Objective: *To recognize and demonstrate movement found in students' natural surroundings*

We can use drama and movement to act out more than just stories and poems. How can you use your bodies to act this out?

Water is made up of tiny pieces called molecules. The colder the temperature, the slower the molecules move. The warmer the temperature, the faster they move. When they are vapour, they move in every direction very quickly, and when they are ice, they hardly move at all.

Five of you will be water molecules. Begin as a group in the centre of the room while the rest of the class chants, "Warming water, making vapour!". To go from water to vapour, you should move in all directions: up, down, and around one another, and eventually to the far ends of the room.

Next, five of you will turn from water to ice. Stay inside a circle on the floor, which is your "cup", while the others chant, "Cooler water, moving slower". Within the circle, move around one another using your arms to splash and bump into the sides of your cup. When one of the others yells, "FREEZE", stop moving until the class begins to chant again with the words, "Warmer, warmer, melting water". Then you can move through each state again.

Real Movements

The children's movements mirror those in their natural surroundings. Cut out the pictures of their movements and glue them in the correct order in the boxes below.

1. a growing seed

2. a withering flower

Real Movements

The children are using their bodies to act out movements in nature. Cut out the natural objects below and glue each one in the box next to the child that is acting like them.

seed   tree   flower   ocean

                              Art Lessons | G.1 & 2

Real Movements

Rain Sounds and Dance

Motivation:

To mimic movement found in the natural world in order to understand the relationship between oneself and one's environment

What to Do:

1 Divide the students into groups of four to six. Then divide each group in half. One half will be the sound makers, and the other half will be the dancers.

2 Ask the students what a rainstorm sounds like. Have the sound makers create a sound collage by snapping their fingers as the rain starts to develop, following with clapping, then slapping their thighs, and finally stamping their feet at different rates across the room. Reverse this sequence to settle the rainstorm. At the same time, have the dancers think about what a rainstorm looks like, and ask them to act it out. They could wave their arms, twirl around, jump, or simply move their fingers.

3 Once all the groups have come up with a sequence of sounds and a dance, allow each one to perform for the class, and have the entire class join in.

Checklists

Checklist: Music

- ☐ I can correctly identify sounds in my classroom.

- ☐ I can identify examples of beat in daily life and in music.

- ☐ I can identify patterns of rhythms in language and in music.

- ☐ I can distinguish between beat and rhythm.

- ☐ I can identify higher and lower-pitched sounds in my environment and in music.

- ☐ I can identify examples of dynamics in my environment and in music.

- ☐ I can identify different tempo in my environment and in music.

- ☐ I know how loudness or softness is achieved in music.

- ☐ I can identify the four families of orchestral instruments.

144   Art Lessons | G.1 & 2

Checklist: Visual Arts

☐ I can recognize and name the primary and secondary colours.

☐ I know that secondary colours are created by mixing primary colours.

☐ I can identify the values of a colour.

☐ I can describe different kinds of lines in art and in my environment.

☐ I can identify the characteristics of symmetrical shapes.

☐ I can identify and describe a variety of textures.

☐ I can distinguish between geometric and organic shapes and forms.

☐ I can identify a variety of art tools, materials, and techniques, and know their proper use.

☐ I can identify the elements of design in a variety of familiar art works.

Checklist: Drama and Dance

☐   I can identify and correctly use drama and dance vocabulary.

☐   I can identify the meaning of symbols used in stories and poems.

☐   I can describe the basic ways in which the body can be used.

☐   I can act out the movements of natural objects.

☐   I can identify some of the key elements in drama and dance.

☐   I can use the vocabulary, tone of voice, and body movements appropriate for a specific character when role playing.

☐   I can describe my own and others' work, using drama and dance vocabulary.

Project Ideas

Frère Jacques vs. Brother John

What to Do:

1 Divide the class into two groups.

2 Choose one group to sing the French version, *Frère Jacques* and the other the English version, *Brother John*.

3 Have the two groups sing in a round. Start with one version and join in with the other after the first verse.

4 After you have finished, talk about the similarities in rhythm of each language.

French:	English:
Frère Jacques, frère Jacques,	Are you sleeping? Are you sleeping
Dormez-vous? Dormez-vous?	Brother John, brother John?
Sonnez les matines! Sonnez les matines!	Morning bells are ringing! Morning bells are ringing!
Din, dan, don. Din, dan, don.	Ding, dang, dong. Ding, dang, dong.

So Many Lines

Materials:

- coloured crayons or markers

What to Do:

1 Identify the types of lines in the picture below by highlighting each with a different secondary colour.

2 Then complete the legend to show which type of line goes with what colour.

Lines

☐ **straight**

☐ **curvy**

☐ **zigzag**

My Book of Textures

Make sure all the samples are the same size, and that they are at least half as big as a sheet of paper.

Materials:

- fabric samples
  (furry, smooth, rough, etc.)
- wallpaper samples
  (bumpy, uneven, soft, etc.)
- stapler and staples
- glue
- scissors
- old magazines

What to Do:

1 Choose five textures you want for your book from the fabric and wallpaper samples.

staple

2 Staple the chosen samples at the edges to make a book (textures and wallpaper samples should all be about the same size).

3 For each texture in your book, find one or more images of objects that have that texture in the magazines.

4 Glue the matching images to the textured pages of your book.

5 Let your book dry. Then present it to your class.

furry texture

Freeze Action Charades

Materials:

- paper and pencil
- bowl / hat / box

What to Do:

1 The teacher writes simple actions on individual pieces of paper (one for every student).

2 Put them into a bowl, hat, or box and have a student pick one out and read it to himself or herself.

3 The student needs to think of a body position that will allow the other students to guess what the action is. The student acting must hold the same position until one of the guessing students calls out the correct action.

4 Each student should act out one action.

Don't forget to include facial expressions!

What Are They Thinking?

What to Do:

1 The teacher reads the storybook beforehand and writes up about four or five thought bubbles. The thought bubbles should express what the characters in the pictures are saying in their head, or their states of being, not the text from the story itself.

Materials:
• paper
• pencil
• scissors
• classic storybook

2 Divide the class into four or five groups.

3 Distribute one thought bubble to each group and have them talk about what it means.

4 Read the storybook in front of the class, pausing on each page.

5 After you have read the text on the page, ask the students what the character in that image would be thinking or feeling. Have them raise their hands when they think the character on the page is "feeling" the inner thought written in their thought bubble.

6 Give each group one page of this or another book and have them come up with their own thought bubbles.

All about an Instrument

In a group of four, think of an instrument that you want to know more about. Make a picture of the instrument using any of the art techniques that you learned during the school year (e.g. printmaking, painting, collage, etc.). Go to the library to find books on your chosen instrument. Paste the picture of your instrument and write a description of it on a large piece of paper or Bristol board. Then present your project to the class.

> *Think about the questions below to help introduce the instrument to your class.*

Questions about the instrument:

- Which family does the instrument belong to?

- What is it made of?

- How does it make sound?

- Can you change the pitch and/or volume of the sound it makes? If so, how?

My Lantern (1)

Did you know that the Chinese use lanterns to celebrate their Mid-Autumn Festival? Have you seen lanterns before? Do you know what they look like? Let's make lanterns together and hang them up to decorate our classroom.

What to Do:

Materials:

- glue
- scissors
- pencil crayons
- glitter
- tissue paper (yellow or orange)

1 Cut along the dotted lines to make the "lantern" and its handle.

2 Fold the "lantern" in half lengthwise, with the dotted lines on the outside.

3 Cut along the dotted lines.

4 Decorate each strip with glitter and crumbled tissue paper.

5 Unfold the paper and glue the ends together.

6 Attach the handle to the lantern with glue.

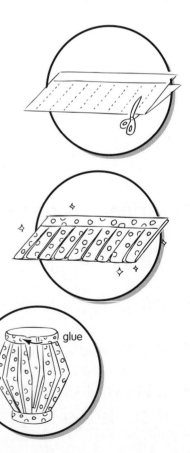

glue

My Lantern (2)

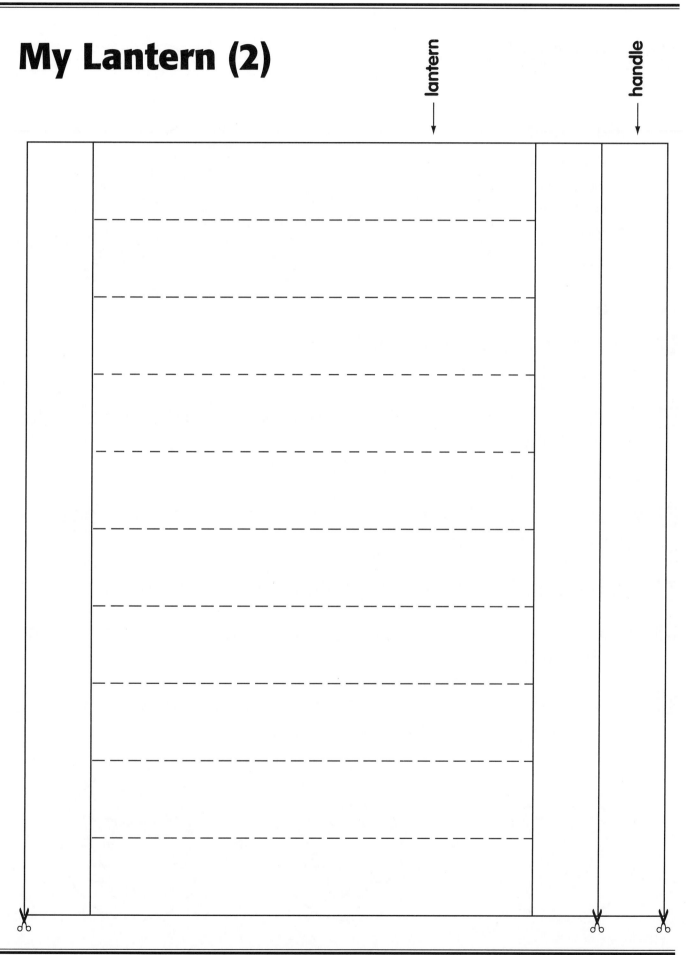

Starry Holder

Materials:

- popsicle sticks
- white glue
- cardboard
- scissors

What to Do:

1 Take three popsicle sticks and make a triangle.
(Make sure that the ends connect but do not overlap.)

2 On top of the triangle, make another triangle so that the triangles form a "star".
(Make sure the star is symmetrical.)

3 Apply dots of white glue at the intersections. Glue popsicle sticks to recreate the first triangle.

4 Repeat step 3. This time, recreate the second triangle.

5 Repeat steps 3 and 4 until the superimposed stars are to the height you desire. Let dry.

6 Trace the shape of the starry holder on the cardboard. Then cut it out and paste it to the base of the holder.

          Art Lessons | G.1 & 2

Colourful Pencil Holder

Materials:

- glue stick
- scissors
- 45-cm-long ribbon
- clean jar
- cellophane in any two primary colours

Do you see the primary and secondary colours on this pencil holder?

What to Do:

1 Cut out pieces of cellophane in each colour, large enough to wrap the jar.

2 Wrap the jar, starting from the base, in the two pieces of cellophane.

3 Secure the wrapping at the opening of the jar with the ribbon.

Primary and Secondary Colours

Look at the colours of the cellophane on your jar and answer the questions.

- What are the two primary colours of cellophane?

  _____

- What is the secondary colour that they create?

  _____

Performing Arts Centres (1)

Performing Arts Centres come in many shapes and sizes, from small concert halls to large opera houses. Despite their many differences, however, they all carry out one simple purpose: to let audiences enjoy performances of the arts. There are many performing arts centres around the world. Below are some of the most famous ones.

Opéra National de Paris

- Paris, France
- opened in 1875
- seats about 2200 people

Sydney Opera House

- Sydney, Australia
- opened in 1973
- has a seating capacity of over 2500

Royal Albert Hall

- London, England
- opened in 1871 by Queen Victoria
- has a capacity of over 5000 including standing in the gallery

Performing Arts Centres (2)

What to Do:

Find a picture of a performing arts centre. It can be from a magazine or a newspaper, or even a picture that you have taken yourself. Paste the picture on a sheet of paper and write something you know about the building. Share your knowledge of the building with the class.

I'm writing about a theatre that is only a few blocks away from my house.

I'm going to find some books about a theatre in Brazil.

Answer these questions to learn more about the performing arts centre:

- Where is it located?

- When was it built?

- How many seats are there for the audience?

- What are some interesting facts about this building?

...nal Puzzle

Choose your favourite animal from the three animals provided. Draw it out on the large grid to see how a picture is enlarged. Then colour the picture and cut it into nine small squares to make a puzzle. Ask a friend to put the puzzle pieces back into place.

Animal ———— My Puzzle

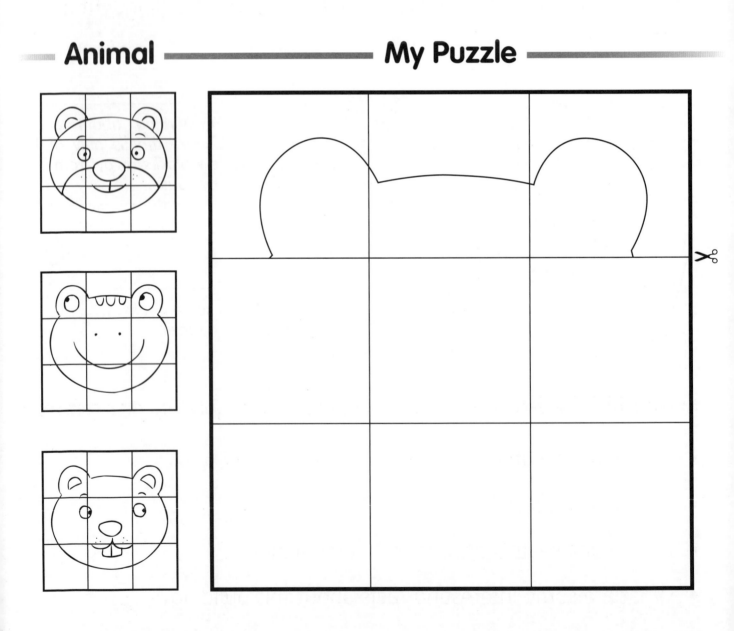